CREATOR GOD, EVOLVING WORLD

CREATOR GOD, EVOLVING WORLD

CYNTHIA CRYSDALE AND NEIL ORMEROD

Fortress Press
Minneapolis

CREATOR GOD, EVOLVING WORLD

Unless otherwise noted, scripture quotations are the author's own translation or
from the New Revised Standard Version Bible, copyright © 1989 by the Division
of Christian Education of the National Council of Churches of Christ in the USA,
and are used with permission.

Parts of chapter 2 are revisions taken from Cynthia S. W. Crysdale, "Making a
Way by Walking: Risk, Control, and Emergent Probability," *Théoforum* 39 (2008):
39–58. Portions of chapter 6 are revisions of previous work in the following arti-
cles: Cynthia S. W. Crysdale, "Making a Way by Walking: Risk, Control, and
Emergent Probability," *Théoforum* 39 (2008): 39–58; idem, "Risk Versus Control: Grounding a Feminist Ethic for the New Millennium," in *Themes in Feminist
Theology for the New Millennium (III)*, ed. Gaile M. Polhaus (Villanova: Villanova University Press, 2006), 1–22; and idem, "Playing God? Moral Agency in an
Emergent World," *Journal of the Society of Christian Ethics* 23 (2003): 398–426.

The diagram of the Krebs cycle on p. 33 is copyright © 2008 Clarke Earley and
used with the permission of the author.

Cover design: Justin Korhonen

Library of Congress Cataloging-in-Publication Data
Crysdale, Cynthia S. W., 1953–
   Creator God, evolving world / Cynthia Crysdale and Neil Ormerod.
      p. cm.
   Includes bibliographical references and indexes.
   ISBN 978-0-8006-9877-5 (pbk. : alk. paper) — ISBN 978-1-4514-2643-4
(ebook)
   1. Religion and science. 2. Evolution. 3. God (Christianity) 4.
Evolution—Religious aspects—Christianity. I. Ormerod, Neil. II. Title.
   BL240.3.C7485 2013
   231.7'652—dc23
                              2012035079

The paper used in this publication meets the minimum requirements of American
National Standard for Information Sciences—Permanence of Paper for Printed
Library Materials, ANSI Z329.48-1984.

Manufactured in the U.S.A.
17 16 15 14 13 1 2 3 4 5 6 7 8 9 10

To John Haughey, S.J. and Patrick H. Byrne,

who encouraged us in the asking of big questions

Creation is not an event but a relation.

—CHARLES C. HEFLING

CONTENTS

CONTENTS

PREFACE

CYNTHIA CRYSDALE

I don't remember when exactly I met Neil Ormerod. It must have been at one of many conferences on theology or Lonergan or both. What I remember is that I quickly pegged him as someone I needed to talk with as much as possible. Once we began corresponding with each other I took every possible opportunity to pick his brain on whatever I was trying to figure out when I happened to encounter him. Between his scientific knowledge and his thorough grasp of the work of Bernard Lonergan, he was always a few steps ahead of me in putting together cutting-edge ideas.

After a few conversations of this sort over several years, I had occasion to visit Neil in Sydney. My daughter, Carolyn, was in a study-abroad program at the University of New South Wales. While I was visiting her in Sydney, Neil graciously drove me to see the Blue Mountains (which in fact I never saw—fog surrounded us the entire time we were there) and he and his wife, Thea, hosted Carolyn and me at their home in Sydney one evening. Neil also invited me to give a lecture at The Australian Catholic University and videocast it to other campuses of the ACU around Australia. After my lecture on the ethics of risk, in which I offered many examples from biology and evolution, he asked me, "Why don't we write a book together on these issues?" I was of course flattered and also thrilled at the prospect of ongoing robust conversations with Neil. I had never done such co-authoring before but he assured me that we could each write sections, comment on each other's work, and then have "Skype dates" for further conversation.

This is exactly what we have done and we would both agree that it has been an exciting challenge and a fruitful exchange. Early on, Neil indicated that I was not to worry about his ego, and we both got used to lots of "tracked changes" interrupting and coloring up our drafts. He would correct major and minor points I made, both scientific and philosophical. I in turn pressed him to think more deeply about several of his positions. We added examples to illustrate each other's arguments. Neil's facility with physics and my longstanding interest in biology meant we each had our teaching moments as well as a wide selection of illustrations to offer one another.

The result of these fruitful interchanges is this current work. We take on big ideas, pushing ourselves to think big thoughts about mostly incomprehensible ideas (like God and the unfolding universe). Incomprehensible does not necessarily mean unintelligible, however, and we have striven to make sense of complex processes and concepts, providing as many examples, illustrations, and stories as possible in order to facilitate insights for readers. However much we have worked to do this and to communicate with clear prose, note that even if you "get it"—whatever the "it" is in any given chapter—your brain is likely to hurt when you are done. This won't be because we are intentionally trying to be erudite or obscure but because the ideas themselves involve considering things too big and too vast to comprehend in a single act.

So what is the big idea here? Or, as I often ask my students at the end of a class, What's the take-home message? One is that the presumed polarity between meaning, purpose, and order on the one hand, and chance, chaos, and contingency on the other, is a misconstrued dilemma. Chapter 2 takes on this false dichotomy by examining two ways science makes sense of the world. Classical science deals with the orderly and regularly occurring phenomena while statistical science asks how often various events occur, yielding probabilities. In fact, chance and order interact as the world unfolds, both contributing to the stable routines and the novel realities that emerge. In essence, even though the theory of evolution introduced the notion of "chance" into what was assumed to be a fully determined world trajectory, chance is not nonsense. Creation—everything in space and time—is part of a continually unfolding interaction between regularities and probabilities. Creation unfolds according to what Bernard Lonergan calls "emergent probability."

A second key idea has to do with how we think about a Creator God. Once we have accepted the role of chance in the unfolding of world process, what do we make of our traditional notions of God as omniscient, omnipotent, and unchangeable? Is God also subject to chance? To the uncertainty of what comes next? In chapter 3 we promote a resounding "no" to these questions. Instead, we retrieve and endorse the classical theism of the Christian tradition. God is fully transcendent, "outside" space and time, and yet fully involved as the primary cause of all that is. A few key distinctions here, most notably between primary and secondary causality, and two different ways of understanding the "contingency" of the world, as well as a clear presentation on the space-time continuum, reveal that the classical conception of a fully transcendent Creator is not only compatible with modern science but indicated by it.

Having made a case for how the world in fact unfolds and for the compatibility of a fully transcendent God with this process, many further questions need to be addressed. Chapters 4, 5, and 6 deal in depth with the implications of our position. Chapter 4 returns to the question of whether there is any purpose embedded in the way the world unfolds; has the introduction of chance into our view of the world meant the death of "teleology"? Chapter 5 addresses the notion of God's providence. Chapter 6 explores further implications for how we understand the challenge of human agency.

For the most part, our approach goes against the grain of most recent science-and-religion discourse in the academy. Whereas most in the science-and-religion community assume that the days of alluding to "Being" are long past, to be replaced by categories of "Becoming," we insist that Being (and such lofty areas such as ontology and metaphysics) are still very much relevant to the questions of our day. We are not in the business of nostalgia, nor of advocating a return to medieval thought and categories. Nor do we endorse any of the new "creationisms" such as intelligent design. Nevertheless, we insist that a transposition of some of the ideas from classical theism, with strong hints from Lonergan's engagement with modern scientific method, are not only worthy of our efforts but necessary for our times. Further, we assume a critical realism—that is, that we can ground our positions in "the ways things really are"—not as a fruit of naïveté but as a result of what Lonergan would call "generalized empirical method." Our positions warrant attention because they make a difference in the world as it exists and unfolds.

We have struggled to generate explanatory categories and this has led us to use critical reasoning and discursive language that may seem alien to the lives of religious believers. Nevertheless, our ultimate goal is pragmatic, that is, to shed light on issues that are often confusing for the generally educated reader. Ultimately, we have set our sights on the ordinary person in the pew, not because we expect her to become an academic in order to believe, but because the issues we raise have exceedingly strong import for how we understand and live within a religious worldview in tune with the contemporary world. Reading this book might leave your brain hurting but it will be well worth the effort in expanding your faith vision.

We owe a debt of gratitude to many who have contributed directly or indirectly to this project. First and foremost we want to thank the seminary students and staff at the School of Theology of the University of the South, Sewanee, who read and discussed our chapters in draft form. In particular we are indebted to Mollie Roberts, Laura Beck, Julia McArthur, Rachel Bush-Erdman, and Mary Ann Patterson. Their engagement with the issues in light of their own faith experiences raised important questions and contributed directly to revisions of our work. Mollie Roberts also did further work as a research assistant and provided helpful editorial advice. Our institutions have supported our work so we render gratitude to the University of the South, Sewanee, as well as to the Australian Catholic University.

Several institutions supported sabbatical and research work for me. My work on creation and evolution began with a sabbatical from The Catholic University of America. St. Jerome's University in Waterloo, Ontario, hosted me as a visiting scholar for this sabbatical and very graciously continued offering me office space in subsequent summers. Christine Schwendinger, Myroslaw Tataryn, and Cristina Vanin were especially helpful in this regard, as were the Masters of Catholic Thought students who took my course on creation and evolution. Ted Laxton in particular has provided feedback on my work. Finally, the Conant Fund of The Episcopal Church has funded summer research and travel to the Galapagos Islands in support of my work.

Both Neil and I are of course indebted to the significant others who support the whole of our work and careers and have been particularly encouraging of this project, most notably Thea Ormerod and Peter Hunter.

We hope that you will enjoy the challenge of encountering big ideas as much as we have.

CHAPTER 1

GOD, RELIGION, AND SCIENCE

A *Family Circus* cartoon shows a young girl, Dolly, asking her father, "If we send astronauts to Mars, do they hafta drive past Heaven?" While this may strike us as funny, it illustrates the double world in which many of us live. Few educated adults would ask such a seemingly simplistic question. Yet many people live in a bifurcated world in which they have accepted the results of science and presume the reasonable world of scientific endeavor, but, when it comes to thinking about God, their worldview may still be somewhat childish, antiquated, or rudimentary. In the scientific world everything is open to question and results are only as valid as the evidence that supports them. With regard to God, however, both believers and nonbelievers often assume that religious issues can only be settled by reverting to a kind of mythic fideism, belief held in contradiction to reason.

The relationship between science and religion has been long, complex, and at times quite conflictual. While everyone knows about the conflict between the scientist Galileo and the Catholic Church of his day, few know that the Vatican now runs its own observatory and there are priests and ministers with international standing in the scientific community. It remains a commonplace in our media to present science and religion as opposed, a position promoted by those on both sides of the issues. There are scientists who love to portray religion as based on superstition and ignorance; and there are believers who cling to fundamentalist readings of Scripture, particularly of Genesis, and so reject modern scientific theories such as evolution. Then there is the broader public caught in the middle, those who appreciate the technological progress made by scientific advances and may in fact seek to maintain some form of religious commitment, but are caught in the pull and counterpull of a debate that they struggle to get a proper handle on.

It is to this middle ground that we direct this book. While it will engage with various aspects of the current debate on science and religion, it is unlikely to convert the scientist who insists that science has disposed of God. Nor will it shift a fundamentalist who wants to maintain that the opening chapters of Genesis provide us with an empirical account of what happened in the first six days of creation. Our task is a more constructive one, of providing a genuine alternative to a number of current approaches to questions around God, creation, and evolution. While we will illustrate our approach with examples from contemporary scientific theories, at the heart of this constructive approach is an intellectual tradition that draws on the best of Christian theology and philosophy.

Central to this tradition is an understanding of God as the transcendent cause of the created order. This position, which contemporary theologians increasingly question, nonetheless provides an account of the relationship between God and creation that is best suited to current scientific understandings of the cosmos; at least that is what we shall argue. Before we get there, however, we shall review elements of the history of the relationship between science and religion to highlight the major themes that we shall need to address.

THE EMERGENCE OF MODERN SCIENCE

Human beings have puzzled over the night sky perhaps from the dawn of human history. What are these lights in the sky? Why do they appear to be in such fixed patterns? What are those lights that wander through the otherwise fixed patterns, those "planets" or wanderers of the night sky? What about the sun and the moon? How can we make sense of these phenomena? These were not idle questions for societies that needed to know the timing of the spring and fall equinox and the winter and summer solstices. These events also had a religious significance in many societies. At least here primitive science and religion had a common interest.

The first serious attempt to respond to such questions was the system devised by the Greek thinker Ptolemy (83–161 CE), which placed the earth at the center of the cosmos, with the sun, moon, planets, and stars rotating around the earth in circular orbits. Of course, it was difficult to fit this model with the actual observations of the planets, in particular, so the model was refined over time to include variations called epicycles to account for the rather odd behavior of the planets. Nonetheless, despite these ad hoc elements, it remained the dominant understanding of the cosmos (in the West) until about the sixteenth century. The first major assault on the Ptolemaic system came from Nicholas Copernicus (1473–1543), who proposed a system whereby the earth and other planets orbited the sun (the heliocentric model).[1] Copernicus maintained the notion of circular orbits around the sun, but to do so required even more epicycles than the Ptolemaic system to match the data. Inspired by new philosophical emphases on empirical observation, the Danish astronomer Tycho Brahe (1546–1601) gathered enormous amounts of precise empirical data on the movements of the planets. Noting the difficulties in fitting this data to the Ptolemaic system, Brahe developed a more complex system in which the sun orbits the earth, while the planets orbit the sun. His assistant, Johannes Kepler (1571–1630), pushed this further to suggest that in fact the sun was central with the earth and planets in orbit around it. Drawing on the empirical data that Brahe produced, Kepler derived a number of laws of planetary motion. Among other things, these specified that the orbits were not perfect circles, as Copernicus had suggested, but ellipses. These were remarkable conclusions to draw from the empirical data and required painstaking calculations. Galileo (1564–1642) added to the picture with empirical observation from more powerful telescopes, providing further evidence of the heliocentric model. In his observations of the planet Jupiter and the discovery of its moons he found a model in miniature of the solar system as a whole.

It was not the intention of these men to provoke a conflict between science and religion. Each grew up in cultures where religious belief was taken for granted. But the religious world of the time was strongly tied to a Ptolemaic cosmology. Indeed, even we moderns need reminding at times that the earth is not the center of the universe. This Ptolemaic model was roughly congruent with biblical cosmology and was entrenched in a certain metaphysical view of the world.[2] Disentangling these religious, scientific, and metaphysical questions was never going to be easy, nor is it necessarily any easier today, as we shall see. The conflict was perhaps as inevitable as it was regrettable, and came to a head most famously in the clash between Galileo and the Catholic Church.

This conflict, however, did little to slow the march of science, with the decisive breakthrough emerging in the work of Isaac Newton (1643–1727). Newton supplied what those prior to him lacked, a new mathematics equal to the task: calculus. With his three laws of motion, including the law of universal gravitation, and his newly invented mathematics, Newton was able to derive the elliptical orbits of the planets and Kepler's other laws.[3] The heliocentric model was now not just a matter of observation; it fit within a mathematical and scientific framework that had explanatory power. This marriage of empirical observation and mathematical formulation was the decisive breakthrough that has become central to our modern conception of science. Newton set the benchmark for all future development in science.

NEWTON AND GOD

Of course, Newton saw no conflict between science and religion. He was a deeply religious person, though of unorthodox persuasion.[4] When he wrote his most famous work, the *Principia mathematica*, he conceived of it as a work that would contribute to natural theology, that is, a philosophical argument for the existence of God: "The most beautiful system of the sun, planets, and comets, could only proceed from the counsel and domination of an intelligent and powerful Being. . . . This divine Being governs all things, not as the soul of the world, but as Lord over all . . . the true God is a living, intelligent and powerful being."[5] The wonders of the cosmos, revealed through scientific discovery, would lead people to acknowledge the existence of God. It is a strategy some would like to promote today. However, Newton had another, more practical reason to evoke God. His account of the solar system had a major difficulty, one that he felt could be solved only by invoking God's action.

When we consider the movement of two objects under Newton's laws of motion, such as the sun and the earth, then an application of the calculus can demonstrate that the orbit will follow an elliptical path, as Kepler had calculated empirically. If you have three or more bodies, however, the problem is more complex. Then each body attracts every other body in some way. Where one body, the sun, is much more massive than the others, certain simplifications can be made, but the problem is still very difficult. Each of the planets perturbs the orbits of the other planets. Why is it that these perturbations do not cause the whole thing to collapse or send the planets flying off into interstellar space? Mathematically, the problem was too hard for him to solve. Instead, he postulated intermittent divine interventions to ensure the stability of the solar system. For Newton, when a gap in scientific explanation appears, one can appeal legitimately to God's intervention. Thus, with the emergence of modern science, we witness also the emergence of the "God of the gaps" strategy.

It is important to pause here to grasp the larger significance of this move on Newton's part. An earlier Christian tradition spoke in terms of primary and secondary causes. God is the primary cause of everything, but God acts through secondary causes (which we might think of here as "laws of nature"). While the tradition allowed for certain special divine interventions in the form of miracles, these were extraordinary events. By evoking God to resolve the difficulties of the stability of the solar system, Newton was also evoking God as a secondary cause whose regular divine interventions are needed to keep the whole system stable. God was now the explanation, not just of the whole, but of certain parts of the whole. It was a strategy fraught with difficulties.

These difficulties emerged with the work of French mathematician and physicist Pierre-Simon Laplace (1749–1827), sometimes referred to as the French Newton. With more refined mathematical analyses, Laplace made some progress on the issue of the stability of the solar system. His results were published in his *Mécanique Céleste*, a work that took Newton's achievements to a new level. Laplace presented a copy of his work to Napoleon Bonaparte (himself something of an amateur mathematician), who commented that the work contained no mention of God. Laplace responded, "I have no need of that hypothesis."

Of course, the problem of the stability of the solar system is far more difficult than Newton or Laplace could imagine. Another great French mathematician, Jules Henri Poincaré (1854–1912), in fact demonstrated that the general system is mathematically unstable or chaotic. Be that as it may, the positions of Newton and Laplace set a pattern for subsequent debates on the relationship between science and religion. Is God not only a primary cause but also a secondary cause, intervening occasionally to ensure God's order in the universe? Alternately, does the advance of science render God obsolete, an unnecessary hypothesis? We can hear echoes of this in current debates over "intelligent design."[6]

THE "NEWTONIAN" WORLDVIEW AND DEISM

There was a further implication that could be drawn from Newton's success that Laplace was willing to draw. Newton's mathematical laws of motion are "deterministic" in the sense that they provide a model of causation where effect necessarily follows from its cause. There is a direct relationship: if A, then B. For Laplace this meant that if one knew the position and velocity of all the particles of the universe, then using Newton's laws one could know the past and the future with absolute certainty. We would live in a completely determined universe, which was then imagined like a huge machine, or clock, which operated according to fixed laws whose outcomes were absolutely certain. There is some irony in Laplace adopting such determinism because he was also one of the founding figures of mathematical statistics. But for Laplace such statistical methods were needed not because the universe was indeterminate, but because of the limits on our knowledge.

This deterministic "Newtonian" worldview was an interesting mix of science and philosophy with important religious consequences. On the one hand, God was thought of as a supreme watchmaker, who established the universe to operate according to its fixed and immutable laws, to produce a universe with a completely determined future known to God. God knows the future with absolute and mathematical certainty, and so sets the initial conditions of the universe to unfold exactly as the divine will wishes. God can then be viewed as the sovereign Lord of all creation. On the other hand, since the laws of physics determine the unfolding of the universe completely, there is no room left for divine intervention, miracles, or divine revelation in human history. And so we see the birth of Deism, a religious position based on reason rather than revelation, with an all-knowing God who is disallowed by the very establishment of the universe from intervening in it. Given the historical circumstances in Europe at the time, with continual conflicts between differing versions of Christianity, it was an appealing stance for many thinkers.

There is a powerful convergence here between two distinct ideas, one metaphysical, the other scientific. Christians had long held that God was all-powerful and all-knowing. If God is all-powerful, then what God wills to happen necessarily happens. This is a metaphysical position. It is all too easy, however, to marry this metaphysical stance with the determinism or mechanical necessity of the Newtonian worldview. This then becomes the great era of the "argument from design," of which religious apologists at the time were so fond. They drew a straight line from the evidence of design in nature to the necessity of the laws of nature to the necessity of the divine will and hence the existence of God. It was a powerful mix. At the religious level, however, it was hardly a religion to warm the heart. The God of Deism is remote and uninvolved.[7] Having set the universe in motion, the God of Deism has nothing more to do or say to humanity. And the deterministic conclusions sat at odds with any notion of human free will. In the face of this rationalism, many Christians adopted an intense inner piety, not quite sure what to make of the world at large.

BEYOND THE NEWTONIAN WORLDVIEW: DARWINISM AND QUANTUM MECHANICS

To some extent the Newtonian worldview still dominates our imaginations in relation to the world. We still hanker for a world of "If A, then B." For example, it took decades for the tobacco industry to admit that smoking causes lung cancer. They would repeatedly claim that the relationship was "only" statistical. Many people who smoke do not get lung cancer, so how can it be a cause? Similar arguments arise on the relationship between pornography and sexual violence. Does pornography lead to sexual violence? Many people view pornography and do not commit acts of sexual violence. But that does not mean that there is not a statistical relationship. We have trouble recognizing and accepting this form of statistically causal relationship.

In the scientific world, however, the determinism of the Newtonian worldview suffered a major blow, not initially in the area of mechanics, but in biology. In the nineteenth century scientific interest grew in the question of life and its diversity. How do we account for the rich diversity of life forms that we find on our planet? Was that diversity there from the beginning? Then how do we account for the various similarities we find across all the variety? Different attempts were made to develop a scientific response to these questions, but the one which struck the deepest chord was that proposed by Charles Darwin (1809–1882). Following his voyages on the HMS Beagle, Darwin wrote his famous work *On the Origin of Species*, where he proposed an account of the evolution of species through species variation and natural selection. Though he himself may not have seen it, both these principles are inherently statistical in nature. Species variation will occur with a certain probability, "every so often." Later developments in biology will refine this by a consideration of random mutations in the genetic code, something of which Darwin was unaware. There is no way of predicting when such mutations will occur or what impact they will have. Natural selection is also statistical in nature. The fittest progeny are more likely to survive and have offspring. But how likely is "more likely"? Again, a statistical analysis is required.

In terms of its impact on biology, Darwin's theory of natural selection has been as significant as Newton's laws of motion for physics. It has added to the empirical data an overarching theoretical perspective that has explanatory force. Without such an overarching perspective the science of biology would simply be data gathering, classifications, and descriptions of living things. With the theory of evolution biological scientists could begin to understand the relationships between living things. Adding modern genetics to the picture creates a powerful construct. This is not to say that it is the final word in biological science. Just as Newton's law of universal gravitation has needed to make way for Einstein's theory of general relativity, which in turn may need to make way for some future quantum theory of gravitation, so Darwin's theory may need to make way for a more refined theory that has greater explanatory force. But despite this, just as Newton's law of gravitation is good enough for most problems in celestial mechanics as a first approximation, so, too, Darwin's theory of evolution will remain a good first approximation to whatever replaces it. It is the best explanatory account we have at present.

Of course, people generally focus on the religious impact of Darwin's theory of evolution in relation to a fundamentalist reading of Genesis. Clearly the two are incompatible, but for many Christians the problem is easily resolved by moving away from a literal reading of Genesis. As far back as St. Augustine (354–430), people had recognized the problem of using the Bible to extract scientific truths and had drawn a distinction between the truths of salvation and those of science. Augustine noted that "whether heaven, like a sphere, surrounds the earth on all sides as a mass balanced in the center of the universe, or whether like a dish it merely covers and overcasts the earth" is not something that the Scriptures determine.[8] In a similar vein the *Catholic Encyclopedia*, published in the first decade of the twentieth century, could find no objection to the theory of evolution on the basis of faith: "It is in perfect agreement with the Christian conception of the universe; for Scripture does not tell us in what form the present species of plants and of animals were originally created by God."[9] What was more difficult for some was the breakdown that Darwinism had for a Newtonian worldview with its marriage of divine omnipotence and deterministic science. If biological evolution involved chance, then God could not be involved, or at least so some concluded.[10] It is a chorus we still find in contemporary writings, such as those of scientist Richard Dawkins.[11]

Again, we find a heady mix of science, metaphysics, and religious belief. If religious belief in divine creation is equated with a deterministic worldview, then evolution is a deadly blow. If the world is not deterministic and we wish to maintain belief in God, can God still be a provident and omnipotent Creator? Faced with such a dilemma many theologians have adopted a "process" understanding of God, no longer omnipotent or supremely provident, more a benign presence influencing the universe.[12] Like Laplace's conclusion of a philosophical determinism from Newton's laws of mechanics, Darwin's original biological theory has now spilt over into a metaphysical account of the world, a total worldview in which chance rather than mechanistic determinism rules the roost. And just as Laplace's determinism found its home among both atheistic and religious thinkers, so, too, an evolutionary worldview has been embraced by both atheistic and religious thinkers. It will take some effort to untangle the various threads of this debate.

Of course, a determined determinist could still argue that the statistical elements in Darwin's theory are there only because of our incomplete knowledge. Laplace's account could still hold, assuming we could have complete knowledge of all the particles and velocities in the universe. In that case the use of a statistical method would just be a sign of our ignorance. The real challenge to such a position arises in the heart of Newton's own land, in the physics of the very small. While Newton's laws are very good at telling us about planets and cars and planes, it begins to break down when applied to very small things like electrons and protons. At that level, a different type of mechanics is needed, that is, quantum mechanics.

While there are different formulations of quantum mechanics, perhaps the best known is that of Erwin Schrödinger (1887–1961), known as Schrödinger's wave equation. One of its great achievements was its ability to give an account of the various energy levels of the electron in a hydrogen atom. Just as Newton's law provided an explanation of the elliptical orbits of the planet, so Schrödinger's equation provided an explanation of the "orbits" of electrons around the hydrogen nucleus, a problem that had remained unresolved for some time. There is a significant difference between these two achievements, however. Newton's equations allow us to explain precisely the motion of individual particles. Now, while there are competing interpretations of quantum mechanics, one thing they all agree upon is that the wave equation cannot be used to predict the path of individual particles. What it does is provide information on an ensemble of particles. It is a statistical theory that offers probabilities about the movement and location of subatomic particles, not unlike a weatherman predicting the chances of a thunderstorm. A further consequence is that one cannot precisely measure both the position and velocity of a particle (referred to as Heisenberg's uncertainty principle, from Werner Heisenberg, 1901–1976) so that Laplace's dream of predicting the future cannot get off the ground.

There are heated debates as to whether quantum mechanics is a "complete" account. Perhaps it is possible that a more profound theory could predict the path of individual electrons, through hidden variables that control the destiny of individual particles but which themselves are statistically spread. The great physicist Albert Einstein (1879–1955) rejected the statistical interpretation of quantum mechanics and proposed such a hidden variable account.[13] More recently physicist David Bohm (1917–1992) has developed such a theory, but the debate is far from settled.[14] Certainly there is no simple way forward here, and for the working physicist the statistical account is the best working theory at hand. At present, at least, it would seem that there is an irreducibly statistical component in the way the world operates.

If this statistical component is an intrinsic element in the way the world operates, what are the implications for our understanding of God and God's relationship to the world? Must we banish God altogether or amend our version of God, as the process theologians have done? And does acknowledging such a statistical component abolish the insights of Newton into world process? What would a universe be like that operates with both classical deterministic laws such as those of Newton and statistical laws with random variations such as those of Darwin and Schrödinger?

RANDOMNESS, PURPOSE, AND ETHICS

A further complication that an admission of randomness introduces into the life of believers is the question of purpose. Returning once again to the work of Newton, one of his aims was to banish metaphysical hypotheses of purposefulness, or what an earlier scholasticism called "final causes," from scientific explanations. Final causes are responses to the type of question that asks, "Why did this come about?" The question "Why do we have eyes?" is likely to be answered, "In order to see." That is their purpose. But this does not provide us with a scientific explanation of the origin of eyes. When the first living organisms developed a responsiveness to light, was this "in order that" we would later develop eyes? Can the final state present us with an explanation of the process of development? For Christian believers the question arises in terms of God's relationship to creation. Is there divine purpose in creation? Does God "plan" for human beings to emerge out of the processes of creation? Can we explain the process by the end point it achieves? The technical term for this issue is *teleology*.

Of course, in a Newtonian deterministic universe, purpose is written into the initial conditions of the universe. If the initial conditions determine it to be so, then life will emerge exactly as the initial conditions determine it to happen. Teleology is strongly present, because the beginning determines the end. Again, as we noted above, this approach strongly advocated arguments "by design" for the existence of God. If evolutionary theory is correct and the evolution of life is a product of random processes, however, can we still maintain that there is purpose in the process? Dawkins and others would answer "no," that evolution eliminates any sense of purpose to creation:

> Natural selection, the blind, unconscious, automatic process which Darwin discovered, and which we know is the explanation for the existence and apparently purposeful form of all life, has no purpose in mind. It has no mind and no mind's eye. It does not plan for the future. It has no vision, no foresight, no sight at all. If it can be said to play the role of a watchmaker in nature, it is the *blind* watchmaker.[15]

And without purpose in creation, why do we need a God to explain what has no explanation? Life has no larger purpose, it fits into no larger plan. Just adjust to the meaninglessness and get on with your life with stoic determination.

Of course, this dichotomy of purpose and randomness needs closer investigation rather than mere assertion. Is randomness opposed to purpose? This appears to be a common assumption of both those who would use evolution to rule out God and those who would question evolution because of the so-called evidence of design.[16] However, can we not use statistical means to attain well-thought-out goals? Indeed, we do so all the time. Consider the link between smoking and lung cancer. It is well established that smoking causes lung cancer with a certain statistical frequency. We know that if we reduce the rate of smoking in the general public we will reduce the incidence of lung cancer. Suppose we introduce a public-health advertising campaign to reduce the incidence of smoking. Some people will see the ad, others will not. Some people will be moved by the ad to quit smoking, others will not. Some will succeed in quitting, others will not. At each step along the way there will be an instance of statistical causation. In the end, if the campaign is successful we will see a decrease in the number of deaths by lung cancer. We will have achieved our goal using a method full of random processes. And for all our success, we will never be able to point to a single person and say, "Our campaign saved your life," because of the probability-shaped nature of the outcome. Perhaps the dichotomy between randomness and purposefulness is overstated on both sides of the debate.

There is a further implication that arises with regard to the supposed purposelessness of world process. This is the question of morality. If we understand the universe as having purpose written into it by its creator, then morality can be thought of as our conforming to that divine purpose. God had a purpose in creating human beings, "to know, love and honor him in this life and to enjoy his presence in the life to come," as the old catechism would say. Given this approach we understand ourselves as free agents who can conform to that purpose, frustrate it, or reject it altogether. And so we develop a notion of sin. If, however, we reject the notion of purposefulness as something written into the cosmos, what sort of moral code, if any, can claim authority over us? Perhaps our sense of morality is simply the outcome of evolution, itself a random, meaningless process, as suggested by Dawkins.[17] Perhaps we simply need to create our own purpose for life, with moral injunctions such as "Enjoy your own sex lives" or "Don't indoctrinate your children."[18]

The issue of purpose and the possible moral implications adds another thread of complexity to the debate on God and creation. Now we not only have questions of science, metaphysics, and religious belief in the mix but also questions of the source of our moral codes. Do they come from God, from nature, or from reason? Are they objective, written into the very structure of reality in some sense, or purely subjective, a matter of personal choice that in the end is basically arbitrary? This connection between metaphysics and ethics is not new. Charles Taylor has pointed out that, prior to our modern era, the primary sources for people's moral frameworks were metaphysical, particular assumptions about the metaphysical ordering of the world.[19] One's moral responsibility flowed from his or her place within the larger scheme of things. The Catholic tradition of natural law also makes a strong connection between metaphysics and morality. If one wants both to maintain a role for God as the sovereign Creator of the universe, and to accept that the world unfolds not in a deterministic manner but with a considerable amount of randomness, what are the implications for our understanding of moral action in the world?

AUTHORITY, TRADITION, AND REASON

It is worth noting at this stage something of the cultural impact that the emergence of modern science has had on our world. In fact, this impact is part of the larger picture of the tension that exists between religion and science. In religion there will always be a strong orientation to tradition, which carries with it the authority of a religious founder or text. Christianity in particular understands itself as based on a revelation from God, made manifest in the historical event of the incarnation of Jesus of Nazareth. The person of Jesus, the foundational texts of his early followers, and the institutions which emerged from that initial event have a continued authority within the Christian tradition. Early on, Christian belief found a congenial partner in Greek philosophy. And so a long journey of Christian theologizing was born that sought to bring together faith, which spoke with the authority of religious tradition, and reason, conceived in terms of philosophical reasoning. And even in the arena of philosophical thought there were authoritative figures from the past, such as Plato and Aristotle, whose works were read and commented upon. Indeed, this association of reason with philosophical thought is still evident today in the encyclical of Pope John Paul II, *Fides et ratio*. In that encyclical reason is exclusively discussed in terms of philosophical reason.

Yet, in its earliest forms, what counted as philosophy was a relatively undifferentiated mix of themes, including questions about the nature of existence, of God, of matter, but also concerns about cosmology, physics, and biology. The forms of reasoning were a mixture of logic, of deduction from a priori principles, and of empirical observation. Even at the beginning of the modern era, when Newton wrote his *Principia*, he thought of it as a work in natural philosophy. However, the success of the new empirical methods in conjunction with mathematical formulations in explaining the world has put the older philosophical arguments into the shadows and challenged those who appealed to religious tradition to settle scientific questions.[20] The dispute between Galileo and the Catholic Church was also a heated debate between Galileo and Aristotelian conceptions of the cosmos and the proper form of science.

The fallout of this conflict was to undermine significantly the authority of arguments based on tradition. An emerging Enlightenment mentality rejected appeals to traditional authority and sought to appeal to "reason" alone as having authority over us. It was not a purely philosophical form of reason, however, as was previously the case, but a scientific form of reasoning that could appeal to the empirical data to settle disputes between competing claims—a marked difference from the interminable disputes between competing philosophical and religious claims. With the success of Newton there emerged a raft of other sciences, not just the physical sciences of physics and chemistry but also sciences of the human condition such as economics, sociology, and psychology. These human sciences were often in direct competition to the claims made by religious traditions, in a far more radical way than concerns over the structure of the solar system or even biological evolution.

At one level there is a tension here between two different knowledge claims, one that takes its stand on tradition, ancient authorities, and texts, the other taking its stand on empirical data. One will seek to settle disputes by appeal to the authority of tradition, the other by appeal to empirical evidence. Both are in some sense an appeal to reason, but reason is conceived very differently in these two approaches. The second approach is more egalitarian or "democratic" because the empirical evidence is there for anyone to verify, while the authority of tradition is held by certain religious "experts": bishops, priests, or theologians. At another level, however, it is a conflict between two competing authority systems. The religious expert has been replaced by the scientific expert as a carrier of socially recognized authority. Few "lay" people (that is, nonscientists) have direct access to the workings of scientific methods or could verify for themselves the claims scientists make. The authority of the scientific expert is reinforced by the enormous success science has had in explaining the world. But for many people it is no more accessible than the output of religious "experts." This clash of authority systems adds another dimension to the science-and-religion debate.

A TALE OF TWO AUTHORS

Perhaps nothing expresses the tensions and divergences in the science-religion debate better than the differing trajectories of two leading authors in the field, Paul Davies[21] and Richard Dawkins.[22] Between them they have authored and co-authored dozens of books on scientific issues that in one way or another address questions of creation, God, and religion. Both are scientists with solid international reputations in their respective fields and both have a gift for clearly communicating the complexities of science in a way that nonscientists can understand. Davies is primarily a physicist and cosmologist, but in his more recent writings he has turned increasingly to the question of the origin of life in the universe. Dawkins is a biologist who has become increasingly strident in his opposition to all religion and religious beliefs. Both have a strong commitment to the importance of reason as a primary source of intellectual authority.

While Dawkins has promoted atheism with an almost evangelical fervor, Davies has shifted more and more from a scientific agnosticism in relation to God to being open to the possibility of God's existence. Dawkins seems to suggest that scientists like Davies, who write favorably about religion, may be being lured by the prospect of receiving money from the Templeton Foundation, which has funded or rewarded many efforts to explore the connections between science and religion.[23] However, one could also note that the path Davies walks has a strong intellectual tradition. In fact, it came as no surprise to those familiar with his work to find him writing in an Australian metropolitan newspaper what came close to a traditional argument for the existence of God.[24] Davies raises the question of the success of science in explaining the world—a point Einstein also made when he noted that "the most incomprehensible thing about the world is that it is comprehensible." Indeed, the very success of modern science in all its forms points to the intelligibility of the universe. Davies goes on:

> Science is founded on the notion of the rationality and logicality of nature. The universe is ordered in a meaningful way, and scientists seek reasons for why things are the way they are. If the universe as a whole is pointless, then it exists reasonlessly. In other words, it is ultimately arbitrary and absurd. We are then invited to contemplate a state of affairs in which all scientific chains of reasoning are grounded

in absurdity. The order of the world would have no foundation and its breathtaking rationality would have to spring, miraculously, from absurdity. So [Steven] Weinberg's dictum is neatly turned on its head: the more the universe seems pointless, the more it seems incomprehensible.[25]

Of course, Davies is not suggesting that the universe is absurd. He is suggesting that if the universe has no source in intelligence (God), then the success of science is incomprehensible. Davies is implying that this is somehow offensive to reason itself.

The move here is from the field of science to the field of metascience, or what is more commonly called *metaphysics*. The very success of science in explaining the world cannot be explained by science; one cannot use a scientific method to validate scientific method. One must move beyond scientific questions to metaphysical questions about the very nature of reality. The very success of science seems to imply that reality is intrinsically intelligible and reasonable. If this were not the case, science would not get off the ground. It would be building castles on the sand. For Davies the more successful science is, the more it raises the God question with ever-greater force.

Dawkins, too, is clearly captured by the rationality of science and its success in providing rational explanations for natural phenomena. He, too, can be moved to awe at the power of science. But for Dawkins this awe raises no further questions. The move from science to metascience is disallowed and the success of science is simply a brute fact occasioning no further explanation.

Of course, Davies is not trying to prove the existence of God using science. He is using the success of science to raise the metaphysical question about God's existence. He is aware enough to know that science cannot prove the existence of God. Yet, contrary to what Dawkins promotes so fervently, neither can science render the existence of God impossible or unnecessary. What Davies is suggesting is that a strong commitment to the validity of science is highly congruent with belief in the existence of an intelligent and reasonable creator of the universe. And this is what all people call God, as Aquinas would say.

This is not to say that Dawkins's arguments against religion are without foundation. Christians who insist on a fundamentalist reading of the Scriptures in relation to Genesis do a disservice to faith by splitting faith from reason and pitting science against religion. Many people, if forced to choose between the two, will opt for science because of its more tangible benefits. It is a choice they should never be forced to make. God is the author of all truth, both religious and scientific, so there can be no disjunction between them unless truth is pitted against itself. Nor can attempts to overcome the disjunction by claiming a faith stance as scientific and then forcing the empirical evidence to fit the faith stance, as is done in so-called creation science, be accepted. This is both poor theology and poor science. We can accept the Bible as the word of God without turning it into a scientific textbook. Those who do so provide the enemies of religion with ample ammunition.[26]

This is not the place to address in a systematic fashion all the arguments Dawkins raises in his attack on religion. Others have done so and the reader can profitably turn to these works.[27] The point here is to remind ourselves that a person can be led by science both toward God and away from God. Paul Davies's writings demonstrate an increasing openness to the God question, without abandoning his commitment to science. Indeed, it is his very commitment to science as a rational activity that leads him to raise the question of God. Richard Dawkins, by contrast, has become increasingly vocal in his rejection of religion and God. Much of his argument is that the theory of evolution eliminates any sense of design or purpose in the universe and hence eliminates any argument for the existence of God. He in fact argues that "the Argument from Design, then, has been destroyed as a reason for believing in a God."[28] His commitment to science leads him to conclude that the universe as a whole has no deeper meaning or purpose. There is clearly no necessary leap from science to atheism here.

CONCLUSION

What we have set out in this chapter is the agenda for the rest of the book. The issues of God, science, and creation raise a number of fundamental questions, but these questions need to be carefully unpacked. There are questions that properly belong to the realm of science. There are questions that are properly metascientific or metaphysical. There are basic faith commitments that may relate in some way to these metaphysical problems. And there are also questions about the ethical implications of what emerges in response to these other questions. Getting the questions right and separating out the various concerns is only the start of the process.

Our approach will be largely constructive. That is, the plan is to construct a worldview that is consistent with core Christian beliefs and with the best of modern science.[29] It will draw on the intellectual heritage of Thomas Aquinas (1225–1274) and its modern mediation in the writings of Bernard Lonergan (1904–1984), principally in his book *Insight*.[30] This is admittedly a formidable work and truly ahead of its time. Our own efforts to unpack its implications will only be scratching the surface. But we wager that it will lead us to a better understanding of the issues involved and a clearer resolution than that proposed by others engaging in the present debate.

CHAPTER 2

EVOLVING WORLD: REGULARITY AND PROBABILITY

As a member of the Tennessee Trail Association, I (Cynthia) join a number of avid hikers once a month for a stroll around "The Domain" of the University of the South: thirteen thousand acres on top of the Cumberland Plateau in eastern Tennessee. On one particularly spectacular winter day, I struck up a conversation with a retired gentleman as we walked. I explained that my academic work involves the relation between science and religion, particularly with regard to issues of creation and evolution. "Well, I am pretty sure what I think about that," my walking companion offered congenially. When queried further he threw out his arm in a wide arch, pointing to all the beauty of the woods, mountains, and valleys: "This can't all have been an accident." While he did not elucidate on what he *did* think was responsible for the wonders around us, it was clear that he was in awe of creation, but also that he assumed there were only two alternatives: either it was "all an accident" or someone or something had intentionally created it.

This assumption, made easily enough by a well-educated retired gentleman in Tennessee, is one that a large proportion of the population shares. Either the world has come about "by accident" or there is a purposefulness embedded in it by an intentional being—usually articulated as "God," whatever one's conception of the deity might be. Paul Davies alludes to this commonly assumed polarity in an *Atlantic* article entitled "E.T. and God,"[1] citing Jacques Monod as illustrating the classic position of the scientist who believes that evolution has now shown the universe to be meaningless: "Man at last knows he is alone in the unfeeling immensity of the universe, out of which he has emerged only by chance."[2] In contrast, Davies writes about scientists who believe they have found order and purpose in the universe. Many such scientists refer to the unlikely coincidence of events that would be necessary for the emergence of life on earth. As Davies puts it: "Many scientists believe that life is not a freakish phenomenon (the odds of life's starting by chance, the British cosmologist Fred Hoyle once suggested, are comparable to the odds of a whirlwind's blowing through a junkyard and assembling a functioning Boeing 747) but instead is written into the laws of nature."[3] Davies goes on to add the theological component. Generally, those who would agree with Monod about the purposelessness of the universe exclude the notion of a creator God—hence, the "alone in the universe" mantra. Those who might agree with Davies or Cynthia's hiking companion about order being written into the universe tend to be more sympathetic to a theological worldview. Davies contrasts "sheer chance" with "lawlike certitude": "The theological battle line in relation to the formation of life is not, therefore, between the natural and the miraculous, but between sheer chance and lawlike certitude. Atheists tend to take the first side, and theists line up behind the second; but these divisions are general and are by no means absolute."[4]

The objective of this chapter is to unpack these options of "sheer chance" and "lawlike certitude." Our position is that these two options do not exhaust the possibilities for our attempts to explain the world around us. Indeed, such a polarity is falsely grounded, such that the problems that it raises can be resolved once underlying misconceptions are cleared up. Later chapters will deal with questions of God, creation, and purpose or design. The main point in this chapter is that the introduction of chance into our understanding of how the world unfolds (or has unfolded) does not pose as much of a threat to an intelligible, ordered, even purposeful universe as has been supposed. Chance is not opposed to order and regularity; rather, the two interact in an intelligible, albeit complex, manner that has contributed to the intricacy and magnificence of creation.

TWO WAYS OF MAKING SENSE: CLASSICAL AND STATISTICAL SCIENCE

Since the work of Charles Darwin we have come to realize that certain phenomena in the natural world are not as inevitable and predictable as had been previously assumed. In the world Darwin inherited—that is, the world of Isaac Newton and his newly found laws of physics—it was presumed that everything occurred according to regularity, governed by laws that could be deciphered and turned into mathematical formulas. The image was of billiard balls (or atoms) hitting one another in sequence. When "A" occurs, "B" follows. Science, in this view, is a matter of gradually discovering the sequence of directly causal events that makes the world function. What was new about Darwin's *On the Origin of Species* was that it introduced the idea that there is novelty in the unfolding of world process.[5] Not everything was set in order at the beginning. Instead, we now understand that our world has changed over time, beginning around 13.5 billion years ago in the unimaginable conditions of the Big Bang, through a complex process of galactic and stellar evolution, finally to give rise to the conditions whereby life was able to emerge on our planet. The changes that have come about have been subject to variables that do not operate inevitably but are, in part, chance occurrences. Indeed, there *is* regularity: all things being equal, objects fall when dropped and seeds sprout when planted. But *in addition* to regularity there is probability: the *likelihood* of objects falling or seeds sprouting under certain circumstances.

So today we recognize two types of inquiry that seek to understand the world in two complementary but different ways. Science of the "classical" kind sets out to understand regularities. By examining, in the field or in the lab, instances of particular phenomena, the scientist grasps the possibility of patterns in the data and so proposes a hypothesis or "law" that provides a unified explanation of these events, all other things being equal. These explanations abstract from the particular places, times, and many other aspects of the events that verify them. For example, when Galileo purportedly dropped weights off the Tower of Pisa, he was not concerned with what color they were painted, but in correlating time and the distance fallen; similarly, febrile seizures in children are explained by a failure of the brain's electrical signals due to the sudden onset of a high fever. This explanation ignores the color of the clothes a particular child is wearing, whether her hair is in a ponytail, and how tall she is. The queries of classical science seek to understand systematic relationships between certain kinds of events and their outcomes. In so doing they leave aside what are otherwise merely incidental aspects of these events.

Most of us are familiar with science of this sort and we depend on such explanations and regularities when faced with a crisis in the emergency room or when counting on a pilot to land our plane safely. But note that such regularities and their explanations include the caveat "all things being equal." In other words, regularities depend on certain conditions being fulfilled. So even our dependence on the laws explained by classical science recognizes that the regularities in our world are conditional. That is to say, they are subject to probabilities. Mostly things line up to occasion expected, regular events, but sometimes they do not.

These conditions and whether and when events of a certain kind occur is the work of a different type of science, statistical science. While science of the classical type aims to uncover regularities, those engaged in statistical science seek to understand how often such regularities occur and under what conditions. Thus statistical science treats the same phenomena as classical science but asks different questions. The statistical scientist is not interested in *why* a certain event happens but *how often* it occurs. Thus the first and primary thing done in statistical science is to count events of a certain type under certain conditions. Laws of physics explain why things fall to the ground when they do. But such science does not tell us how likely it is that we will be hit by something falling off the roof of a particular building on a given day. In order to know this we need to count: How often do things fall off the roof, and under what conditions? Do things fall off the roof more often when there has been a heavy snowfall? After a windstorm? On Halloween? So scientists define an event and set a framework in which to count these events. How likely is it that this batter will hit a home run? What is his batting average against this pitcher? Against left-handed pitchers? In the postseason?

Note that the objective of statistical science is to find an *ideal frequency*—the average expected outcome of a set of events. Note also the distinction between the ideal frequency and *actual frequencies*. While the ideal frequency for coming up heads in a coin toss is one out of two, the actual number of times could be seven times in ten throws. This leads to several important points. First, the expected average does not determine what, in fact, the next toss of the dice will yield. Furthermore, actual frequencies diverge *nonsystematically* from the ideal frequency. In a hundred tosses of a coin, it is not the case that every second toss will be a heads while the alternate tosses will be tails. Rather, the actual pattern of heads and tails will deviate from the one-out-of-two average in a random fashion. The same is true of the actual rolls of a dice.[6] In fact, should some systematic pattern appear—say, a consistent run of sixes—one would begin to suspect some interference: Perhaps the dice are loaded?

Now, most statisticians do not spend time calculating probabilities of coin tossing, dice rolling, and card dealing. These calculations, assuming fair tosses and clean dice or decks of cards, can be done with simple math.[7] Most statistical science engages in counting events as they occur in the world. These may be events in the natural world, such as the number of polar bears living in a given year on a certain ice floe in the Arctic. Or it may involve human actions, such as calculating rates of cigarette smoking in a given city during a given year. The point is that one makes sense of these events, not by discovering a systematic set of principles that explains them all, but by counting and calculating probabilities.

These examples allow us to elaborate a few of the differences between classical science and statistical science. First, the object of inquiry is different. While classical science seeks unified explanations that will apply to all similar situations, statistical science aims at finding an ideal frequency, an average number of occurrences of a specified event over against a potential population or a given time or place. Both make sense of the world but in different ways.

Second, while classical science can make sense of individual instances of an event, statistics is always about an aggregate of events. Classical science does depend on aggregates—a number of instances verify a hypothesis about the way things work. If the explanation is correct it will explain each and every instance. Statistical science, on the other hand, can tell us very little about specific events. Knowing the average incidence of lung cancer in a given city does not tell us when or where the next case of lung cancer will occur. It is not that we know nothing; we *do* know the likelihood of polar bears living in the arctic and the likelihood of lung cancer occurring in a population of smokers. But such averages make sense of a group of events and do not indicate exactly where or when the next event of this kind will take place.

Following this, third, classical science sets out to determine the *nature* of some phenomenon while statistical science examines the *state* of things. Classical science is involved in determining, for example, the nature of diabetes, the causes of AIDS, the strain of virus that produces swine flu. But statistical science sets out to determine the state of health in Maryland or Mexico or Burkina Faso: How many cases of diabetes are there? How many people suffer from AIDS? How many people have contracted swine flu? Further refinements yield information about specific populations; the average age, for example, of those with these various ailments.[8]

Finally, note that while these are very different ways of making sense of the world, both classical and statistical science *do* make sense. They both aim at explaining aspects of the world—both of them seek intelligibility (sense rather than nonsense) in the world. Classical science seeks the *intelligibility of system* while statistical science seeks the *intelligibility of probability.*

The importance of this—indeed, the overriding point of this entire section—is to counter the tendency to assume that everything in the world is explained according to systematic processes, that classical science is the only way of making sense of the world. This position assumes that anything that does not make sense in this particular way makes no sense at all. There are systematic, determinate relationships, the "lawlike certitude" that is the object of classical science, or there is "sheer chance," which is unintelligible. In fact, this is not the case. Statistical science does make sense of the world, only in a different way. It yields the intelligibility of probability; this is the making sense of chance. It differs in its questions, its objectives, its answers. But it does make sense of the events that we ordinarily ascribe to chance.

The point here is that "sheer chance" and "lawlike certitude" constitute a false polarity. Many events in the world can be understood according to chance. This is to say, they cannot be explained by a unified account that relates outcomes systematically to a set of causes. But "chance" does not mean "nonsense." There is an intelligibility to chance, albeit a different kind of intelligibility. It is the intelligibility of probability, which is the domain of statistical science.

THE INTERACTION OF CLASSICAL AND STATISTICAL SCIENCE

This explication of classical and statistical science may leave the impression that we live in a bifurcated world and that those who seek to understand it function in two altogether different spheres. While it is important to distinguish the questions, the objects of inquiry, and the intelligibility yielded by classical and statistical science, it is just as important to notice how the two contribute to one another. In fact, scientists regularly confront a certain set of events without knowing ahead of time which type of investigation is warranted. At times they begin an inquiry expecting to find some systematic pattern only to realize that there is no system to be found.[9] They may then shift their endeavors toward counting when and where these phenomena occur.

Likewise, quite often researchers will begin with a count of the conditions under which certain events occur as a clue to what is causing them. By discovering how often certain events occur in different times and place, researchers can begin to explore the root causes of these events.

For example, presume that botanists set out to understand the nature of buttercups.[10] They begin by collecting and classifying different types of buttercups according to height, number of petals, time of blossoming, and so forth. In the process of classifying these buttercups they compare and contrast the number of buttercups of each type that grow in five different meadows.[11] While the expectation is that the distribution of types will show no particular patterns, it turns out that two types of buttercups grow more often in two particular meadows. What was expected to be an even distribution, hovering around a mean, reveals a pattern that indicates some kind of systematic set of relationships. Charted on a graph this would appear as shown in table 2.1.

This pattern leads researchers to embark on a different set of questions, questions that seek to determine what is distinctive about Types A and B in relation to Meadows Two and Three. A comparison of the meadows reveals that the distinctive feature of these two meadows is the drainage of water.

TABLE 2.1

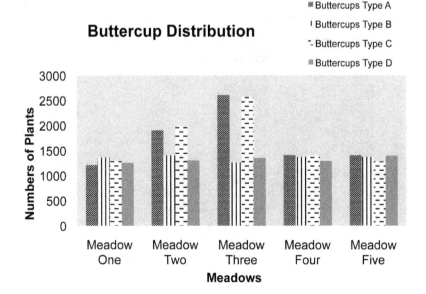

There seems to be some correlation between the flourishing of Type A and C buttercups and land drainage. Further controlled experiments confirm this correlation and help to refine the classifications of these four types of plants.

Another set of examples comes from the work of Peter and Rosemary Grant and their associates. Since 1973 the Grants have studied ground finch populations on a number of small islands in the Galapagos Archipelago.[12] Much of their work has involved the measurement of bird size relative to food consumption. Weight turned out to be an inaccurate indicator of bird size, given daily or even hourly changes. So the Grants and their associates took meticulous measurements of the width, depth, and length of the beaks of the birds they caught in mist nets each morning. In addition, they measured the size and hardness of the seeds available to these birds, coming up with a "struggle index" for different kinds of seeds.[13] They also sampled the number and types of seeds in squared segments of land across the small island of Daphne Major. Eventually, they had enough data to correlate beak size, rate of consumption, and the toughness of seeds that various finch species ate. At first they found that birds of many species and beak sizes ate the same types of seeds. No pattern emerged; finches of different species seemed to partake of their nourishment rather randomly. Table 2.2 shows this.

TABLE 2.2[14]

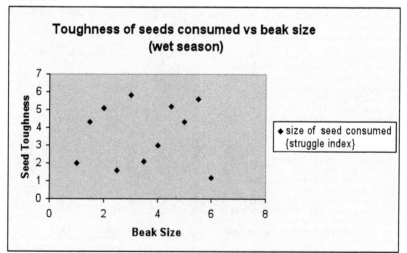

After several seasons visiting Daphne Major during the wet season, when food abounded, the Grants took a hint from a local researcher and returned during the dry season.[15] The abundance of food had disappeared. The birds they had measured just months before had lost weight and the variety of seeds was no longer available. Only the big and tough seeds remained. When observing which birds ate which seeds, a clear pattern appeared. The species with larger beaks were able to crack the larger tougher seeds, while the smaller species had to seek out the tenderer cactus seeds. Table 2.3 illustrates this relationship.

Correspondingly, those with larger beaks were more numerous and more able to survive through the dry season, as in table 2.4.

In the end, it turns out that there is a systematic relationship in finch life between the size of a finch's beak and the type of food it eats. Likewise, there is a relationship between the birds that can survive a drought and those who are lost under such conditions.

The work of one of the Grants' graduate students reveals another way in which statistical population studies can reveal systematic patterns. Trevor Price measured the beaks of all the finch chicks on Daphne Major for a number of years in the late 1970s. By comparing the size of these finches' beaks

TABLE 2.3

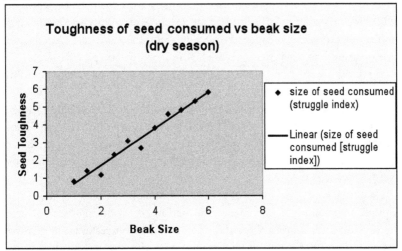

TABLE 2.4

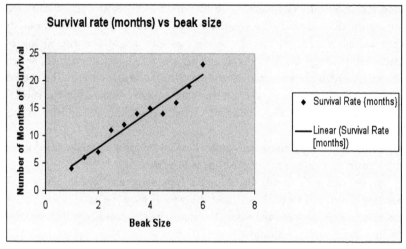

at eight weeks and at eight months he determined that beak size was fixed by eight weeks and changed very little after that. So far he had discovered something about the nature of finches and their life cycles. But Price also counted and calculated rates of survival in the first eight weeks of these birds' lives. In a population of *n* finch fledglings, what percentage died in the first eight weeks of life? All other things being equal, one would expect a straight mathematical average across the population. Yet Price found that his numbers did not revolve around an average but revealed a more systematic pattern. Of all the young birds, the ones who had the narrowest beaks were more likely to survive to adulthood, as in table 2.5.

Hence, the average beak size among this cohort of birds shifted in six months from 9 millimeters to 8.73 millimeters. Generation after generation the same thing happened. As Price writes, "Not every small young finch survived, and not every big young finch died, but the small ones were the most likely to succeed."[16]

We have here a clear case of a statistical finding revealing a pattern that requires some kind of systematic explanation. By counting and calculating survival rates among a specific population, new questions for research emerged. Price quit counting and started observing—what the finches ate, which finches ate which seeds, how their body structure affected what they

TABLE 2.5

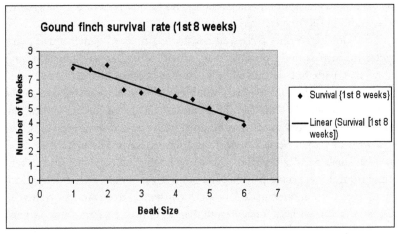

could eat. He eventually came up with a unifying hypothesis that made systematic sense of this statistical finding. The structure of bird beaks at a young age are, like human infants' skulls, very malleable and soft. This is true of both small birds and of the birds with big beaks, which will in adult life be able to crack bigger, harder seeds. The bigger birds with bigger beaks will, as adults, have the advantage of access to a food source unavailable to the smaller birds. At a young age, however, the beaks of all the birds are equally soft and all the young birds depend on smaller, softer seeds to survive. The bigger birds, though, need more food to survive than the smaller birds. In this case, then, the birds with smaller beaks have the advantage since it takes fewer seeds to keep them alive. Thus, it seems, being young and big is a liability in the world of finch fledglings.

IS IT ALL RANDOM?

These examples not only illustrate the interdependence of statistical and classical inquiries, they help to indicate more clearly what is meant by the term *random*. First, there is no such thing as *a* random event. Events can be considered random only in reference to a pattern of events. So there must be an aggregate of instances in which one discerns a trend of some kind. Divergences from this expected trend are random; that is, there is no further pattern or intelligibility to be found in this divergence.

So if one determines a classical law, for example, of bodies moving in a regular orbit, it is quite possible that individual bodies, say asteroids, may follow that path but deviate slightly from it because of interference from other asteroids. These individual "wobbles" will be random relative to the determined orbit.[17] Likewise, in the studies of Galapagos finches we saw that research has revealed a correlation between beak size and seed toughness. The birds with the larger beaks eat larger and harder seeds. The birds with small beaks eat smaller and softer seeds. Now, one might find cases that diverge randomly from this expected pattern. The point is that once one has determined a systematic pattern one can declare specific instances to be random relative to this pattern. But without an aggregate that falls into a pattern, "randomness" cannot be determined.

When it comes to statistical science, randomness is relative to averages found in populations. Thus the average size of a medium ground finch's beak on Daphne Major in the Galapagos in 1976 was 10.68 millimeters long and 9.42 millimeters deep.[18] The actual size of any one finch's beak is expected to deviate randomly from this norm. In this case, the pattern the scientist is

TABLE 2.6

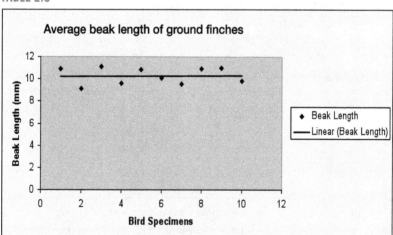

after is the *ideal frequency* among a range of beak sizes. The *actual frequencies* deviate nonsystematically—randomly—from the expected average, as shown in table 2.6.[19] Again, actual cases are random relative to a pattern, but in statistical science the pattern is a mathematical average rather than a systematic correlation.[20]

What follows from this is the fact that there is no such thing as absolute randomness. Randomness is always *relative* to some pattern, whether a systematic correlation (as in classical science) or an average (as in statistical science). To claim that the universe is a completely random affair would require a grasp of some intelligible pattern (a correlation or an ideal frequency) from which all events diverge nonsystematically. But in order to do this one would have to know everything about everything. Patrick Byrne puts it as follows:

> it is impossible to establish by empirical means alone that a given series of events is absolutely random and conforms to no conceivable intelligible pattern. The most that can be established is that the data are random relative to some specifiable (albeit extremely complex) kinds of patterns. To claim that some series of events is absolutely random goes beyond scientific verifiability. It turns a relative into an absolute without scientific warrant.[21]

Once again, the contrast between lawlike certitude and sheer chance turns out to be erroneous. That some set of events is due to sheer chance can only be determined over against the intelligibility of some pattern—either a correlation or an ideal frequency. Without realizing it, then, the hiker in Tennessee was right in saying, "It can't *all* be an accident." To say that evolution is purely random—*merely* accidental—would require absolute knowledge about all possible relationships.

EMERGENT PROBABILITY: ORDER AND NOVELTY INTERACTING

Up to this point the focus has been on inquiry: How do those studying the world make sense of it? We have reviewed two ways of doing this, two types of intelligibility that are sought after in the investigations of classical and statistical science. The further move is to grasp that these two types of intelligibility correspond to two different aspects of world process. There is order and regularity—some things occur in the same way always and everywhere, all things being equal. Other things occur without a systematic pattern or a direct causality but according to probabilities. And just as the two types of inquiry intersect and are mutually creative, so those events that occur according to probabilities (by chance) and those that occur systematically (according to natural laws) interweave to make a stable world process that is nevertheless subject to conditions that change. Bernard Lonergan calls this interweaving of regularity and probability "emergent probability."[22]

To grasp adequately this interaction of regularity and its conditions, one must understand a "scheme of recurrence."[23] If classical science grasps correlations between certain events, it also grasps the fact that the occurrence of some events curl around in a circle, such that, when A causes B, B causes C, which in turn causes A again. Thus a cycle is set up in which the occurrence of any one of these events sets off a recurrent scheme (see fig. 2.1).[24]

Examples of these recurrent schemes abound, from the metabolism of cells in our bodies to the hydrological schemes by which water circulates on the face of the earth. A good example of such a cycle in biochemistry is the

FIGURE 2.1: SCHEMATIC OF A SCHEME OF RECURRENCE

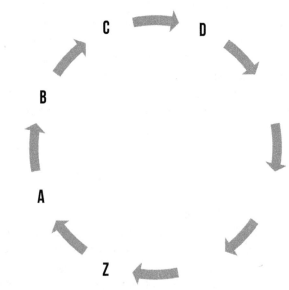

Kreb's cycle (see fig. 2.2). This is the basic scheme of recurrence for energy production in every living cell, consisting of ten distinct steps in the scheme. Hans Adolf Krebs first identified it in 1937, and he was awarded the Nobel Prize for medicine in 1953 for his discovery. It is an excellent example of a scheme of recurrence—in this case a series of chemical reactions—that has been identified and studied in nature.

Further, not only are there single schemes, there are conditioned *series* of schemes of recurrence. So it is that the circulation of water over the face of the earth is a scheme that itself is a condition for the possibility of the nitrogen cycle of plant life to occur. And the nitrogen cycle of plant life is a scheme that is itself a condition for the possibility of the digestive system of animal life to occur. So individual cycles themselves form a conditioned, recurrent series of schemes.[25]

FIGURE 2.2: DIAGRAM OF THE KREBS CYCLE[26]

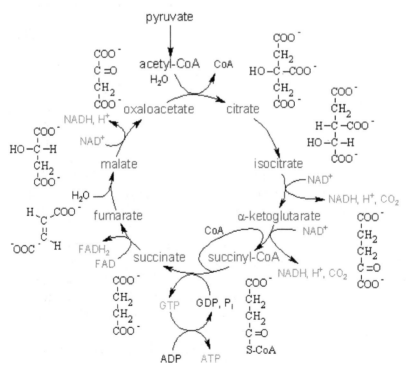

The point is that events that otherwise would remain completely incidental to one another form an integrated whole that establishes stability at a higher level of functioning. So, for example, as in the Kreb's cycle, chemical reactions that at one level are merely coincidental form a scheme of recurrence that establishes cell metabolism at the biological level. Some of these schemes of recurrence, which at the level of biology are merely coincidental, can themselves form cycles of recurrence making sensitive consciousness possible, such that the schemes of recurrence of animal life emerge.

Note that these schemes of recurrence retain their dependence on the underlying manifolds of reactions. So chemical reactions depend on the processes of subatomic physics, and biological processes depend on chemical reactions, and the processes of sensitive consciousness depend on biological processes (which in turn depend on chemical reactions, which in turn depend on physical processes, and so on). Still, the schemes of recurrence that emerge at any level are substantively different from their underlying manifolds. They are not just the sum of their parts. There is a unified whole that is dependent on, but something other than, the reactions upon which they depend.[27]

In the Newtonian worldview of "lawlike certitude," we have the linear image of dominos banging up against one another in succession, directly causal events that occur always and everywhere the same. We need to shift this picture of causality to envision not only chance events (the conditions that make efficient causes possible) but also a pyramid of schemes of recurrence.[28] So, for example, beaks enable finches to grasp seeds so that they can get nourishment that will be turned, through metabolism, into energy to sustain life. But this process depends on the organic schemes of recurrence that make the seeds available. All of these are dependent on climatic conditions, so that when a drought occurs both plant life and bird life are affected.[29] So all of these schemes of recurrence are subject to underlying conditions, and the likelihood of such conditions occurring or not in any given situation is what statistical science can study.

Note how the emergence of new schemes of recurrence dramatically shifts the probabilities of certain further events occurring. When events A, B, and C are merely coincidental to one another, the likelihood that all three will occur together is the product of the likelihood of each event singly. If we assign events A, B, and C the probabilities of 1/3, 1/4, and 1/8 respectively, the chances of all three happening together is the *product* of these chances: 1/3 x 1/4 x 1/8, which equals 1/96 or 0.010 or one chance in a hundred. But if a scheme of recurrence emerges in which any occurrence of event A means that B and C will also occur (and likewise, if B, then C and A, and if C, then A and B), then the likelihood of A, B, and C occurring together jumps to the *sum* of the separate probabilities: 1/3 +1/4 + 1/8, which equals 17/24 or 0.708 or approximately seventy-one chances in a hundred. The point is that with each emergent scheme or system of schemes of recurrence, probabilities of further complexity increase substantially.[30]

This mathematical explanation may make more sense if we turn to an analogy used by Francisco Ayala. He alludes to those critics of Darwin who insist that "random processes cannot yield meaningful, organized outcomes."[31] These critics point out that a monkey sitting at a typewriter hitting the keys at random would never write *On the Origin of Species*, even given millions of years and millions of generations of monkeys. Ayala offers an alternative analogy. Suppose there were a process whereby every time a monkey hit a set of keys that created a meaningful word, this word were selected to make up a different typewriter in which each key was a word rather than a letter. If, then, when a monkey at this second typewriter happened to hit words in sequence that made up an intelligible sentence, these sentences would be shifted to a typewriter in which each key was a sentence rather than a word. He concludes: "If such sentences became incorporated into keys of a third type of typewriter, in which meaningful paragraphs were selected whenever they appeared, it is clear that pages and even chapters 'making sense' would eventually be produced. The end product would be an irreducibly complex text."[32] So it is that the emergence of ever more complex schemes of recurrence makes the likelihood of further developments increase. The world unfolds according to emergent probability.

In debates over evolution, many writers have alluded to the severe unlikelihood of life's emergence in the universe. Given the initial conditions and the precision with which certain variables (such as oxygen in the atmosphere) had to coalesce, the chances that life would emerge are very slim. Some scientists argue that the extremely low probability of life emerging indicates that the life world we inhabit is indeed "just" a matter of chance. Others, such as those to whom Ayala is responding, use such a low probability as an indication that life didn't "just happen" but must have been the product of an intentional designer. In both cases the appeal to chance is misguided since the authors assume that all factors are totally independent of one another.[33] In fact, chance conditions interact with the emergence of schemes of recurrence to yield more and more complex integrations that, in turn, heighten the probabilities of further, more complex integrations.

NATURAL SELECTION AND CHANCE

Another misconception is that natural selection is about random processes. In the (false) polarity between lawlike certitude and sheer chance, Darwin's concept of natural selection has been assumed to be the mechanism by which the world unfolds randomly. A few clarifications with regard to natural selection and its role in evolution are in order.

First, Darwin postulated that just as animal breeders or horticulturalists selectively breed organisms to yield better specimens, nature "selects" the organisms with the most advantageous characteristics. It is these that survive and reproduce.[34] In fact, nature does not "select" anything. Rather, it ought to be considered the process of natural *elimination*. There is no intentional agent picking and choosing among individuals who are fit and those destined to die. Rather, those who have adapted to their environments are the most likely to both survive and reproduce.[35]

Second, natural selection is about populations, not individuals. As Trevor Price indicates in his study of finch fledglings: "Not every young finch survived, and not every big young finch died, but the small ones were more *likely* to succeed."[36] So natural selection is about probabilities, about the *likelihood* of survival and successful mating. In this sense it is about chance. This is not a matter of "mere" chance, however, since systematic explanations can be found as to which traits enhance the likelihood of survival and reproduction and which do not.

Therefore, understanding the evolution of finches in the Galapagos involves determining the likelihood that certain kinds of birds will survive on the island of Daphne Major during a three-year drought. If it turns out that having a large beak is more adaptive—meaning that birds with large beaks are more likely to survive—then it is these individuals who are most likely to reproduce and pass this trait on to the next generation. However, what exactly is "adaptive" depends on correlations that reflect systematic relationships, such as the relation between beaks and seeds. If there were no systematic relationship between beak size and food consumption, then beak size would not be a trait related to survival. Thus natural selection *is* a matter of probabilities, but such probabilities are to be understood, first, as averages over time in a given population in a given place, and, second, as dependent on systematic correlations that relate traits to survival and reproduction.

Third, there *is* a random element here—some aspects of evolution do involve "accidents." But these do not have to do with natural selection *per se*, but with the configuration of underlying traits, the genetic variation upon which the principles of natural selection work. Generally, this genetic variation comes about through three mechanisms: mutation, migration, and genetic drift. *Mutations* are the chance "errors" that occur in the genetic code, either from environmental factors or in the process of reproduction. Most of these changes have little effect on the behavior or traits of the individuals in which they occur. Most often they lead to the demise of the individual who inherits them. Nevertheless, such minor flaws provide the novelty that makes natural selection and evolution possible. *Migration* involves the movement of populations or intersections of populations with one another so that the overall gene pool changes. For example, brown beetles end up "by chance" in a jar of flour with green beetles and start interbreeding. Or snakes live on a peninsula that separates from the mainland, forming an island, so that they can no longer interbreed with the snakes on the mainland. *Genetic drift* involves chance occurrences in a population that have no systematic explanation. For example, someone steps on a group of brown beetles, leaving the green beetles to be more numerous in the next generation.[37]

Ayala offers another example that illustrates these three points.[38] The bacterium *Escherichia coli* needs a certain amino acid, histidine, in order to reproduce in a laboratory culture. Likewise, the antibiotic streptomycin is lethal to most of these bacteria. Under ordinary laboratory circumstances a few bacteria in a small glass tube will multiply in one or two days to produce twenty or thirty billion bacteria. If a drop of streptomycin is added to the culture, all but a few bacteria will die. In a few days, however, the culture will again yield billions of bacteria. This is because spontaneous genetic mutations have left a few cells out of the original millions with a resistance to streptomycin. These few survivors, the ones who are "adaptive" in this new environment, naturally reproduce and in no time there is a large population with this adaptive trait.

Assume, then, that the streptomycin-resistant cells are placed in a culture that lacks histidine. All but a very few will fail to reproduce. But, again, in a few days the culture will be teeming with bacteria. "Natural selection has produced, in two steps, bacterial cells resistant to streptomycin and not requiring histidine for growth. The probability of these two mutations happening in the same bacterium is about four in ten million billion. . . . A 'complex' trait made up of two components has come about by natural processes. . . . Thus natural selection is a creative process, although it does not create the raw materials—the genes or DNA—upon which it acts."[39]

So natural selection is about probabilities of survival and reproduction in populations. But such probabilities depend upon the regular and systematic correlations that explain the type of life being investigated—the relationship between *Escherichia coli*, its ability to survive and reproduce, and the presence or absence of histidine or streptomycin. This involves the interaction of regularity and probability, both of which are subject to intelligible processes that can be explained, and that over time yield different types of organisms and, potentially, more complex schemes of recurrence.[40] The *random* element lies in the "accidents" by which certain mutations enable a small number of cells to survive and reproduce in otherwise fatal conditions.

Thus the appeal to chance in neo-Darwinian evolutionary theories makes a simple and very limited point: that there is no direct causal link between environmental advantage and the origination of heritable traits.[41] The philosopher Patrick Byrne puts it as follows: "the origination of inheritable genetic variations is random relative to their adaptive advantage in the immediate environment."[42] Ernst Mayr, the elder statesman of evolutionary theory, explains it thus:

> The fundamental difference between the first and second steps of natural selection should now be clear. At the first step, that of the production of genetic variation, everything is a matter of chance. However, chance plays a much smaller role at the second step, that of differential survival and reproduction, where the "survival of the fittest" is to a large extent determined by genetically based characteristics. To claim that natural selection is entirely a chance process reveals a total misunderstanding.[43]

CONCLUSION

We began the chapter citing a gentleman who insists that the natural world "can't all be an accident." To the degree that he assumes that there are only two choices—order and accident—this chapter has tried to clarify a misconception.

The polarity between "lawlike certitude" and "sheer chance" is mistaken at its core. What we have instead is two forms of lawfulness, a classical, systematic lawfulness and a statistical form of lawfulness. Several points have been made in service of this clarification. First, to the degree that chance is operative in the world, chance does not imply "nonsense." One can make sense of chance—it is intelligible—but in a way that is not the systematization of classical science. Rather than finding a unified explanation for a whole host of similar events, statistical science makes sense of chance according to the intelligibility of probability. To invoke "certainty" over against "accident" overlooks several centuries in which statisticians have in fact made sense of chance by counting events and calculating probabilities.

A further point is that the world unfolds through the interaction of the regularities and probabilities that classical and statistical science study. There are regularities in the world that occur according to scientific "laws." But these regularities depend on underlying conditions. The interaction of regular efficient causes with the conditions that make them possible constitutes what Bernard Lonergan calls *emergent probability*. The regularities governed by the laws of nature emerge and disappear according to scales of probability. Furthermore, the existence of schemes of recurrence, and series of interrelated schemes of recurrence, heightens the probabilities that systems of irreducible complexity, such as life, will emerge. Thus evolution, including the emergence of life and of human consciousness, is neither a pure accident nor a totally determined system.

At the same time, evolution does involve accidents. Mutations, migration, and genetic drift supply the variation to the gene pool within which natural "elimination" works. Natural selection, then, involves the interaction of probabilities of emergence and survival with systematic correlations that establish which kinds of traits will survive and be passed on to the next generation. So far from an "either/or" of determinism versus chance, world process unfolds in an elaborate interweaving of regularity and probability.

What does all of this have to do with God? We have gone to great lengths to explain how the world unfolds but have not invoked God's action in any of it. If indeed the world emerges in this dance of order and chance, must we then abandon the notion of God as all-powerful and all-knowing? Is God herself caught up in this interaction of chance and necessity? Perhaps God—or at least God's knowledge of creation—is also still "emerging." To these questions we now turn.

CHAPTER 3

CREATOR GOD

At a family gathering recently, I (Cynthia) encountered a long-lost cousin who admitted, with a certain chagrin, that she attended a parish church that recently had cut its ties with the Anglican Communion over theological differences. Given the controversy over sexual orientation abreast in the global church, I assumed that the issues were of a moral nature. Instead, she simply quoted the antagonists with dismay and disdain—"God needs us as much as we need God"—and then commented: "What kind of a faith is that?"

With simple but accurate intuition, this believer put her finger on one of the key issues in our modern conception of God. In the previous chapters we have noted the ways in which our views of the world have radically changed because of the discoveries of modern science. The world emerges from a complex interaction of both classical and statistical forms of lawfulness. Rather than a biblical account of a world made originally complete by God, we now know that the whole universe has evolved over billions of years, and that the emergence of life is part of that larger picture of development and complexification. Many have then argued that because of this change we must also change our understanding of God. In fact, change is the basic issue. If the universe changes so radically, must we also insist that God, too, changes?

To respond to this question we need to consider difficult philosophical questions about the way in which God relates to creation. As indicated earlier, we maintain that the classical understanding of God developed by great figures such as Thomas Aquinas is still viable in the face of the claims of modern science. In fact, we shall see that modern science is more supportive of the classical position than are modern attempts to introduce change into God.

To get to this stage, however, will require the introduction of quite profound notions from both science and metaphysics.

GOD, CONTINGENCY, AND CHANGE

We shall begin with an outline of various theologians and philosophers who have suggested the need to reconceptualize our understanding of God's relationship to creation. The most prominent of these are those who follow the thinking of philosopher Alfred North Whitehead, whose position has become known as *process philosophy* or *process theology*. Many other theologians, however, have similarly struggled with the need to revise our understanding of the God-creation relationship.

Charles Hartshorne, in his Aquinas Lecture of 1976, summarized the basic position of process thought as follows:

> The entire history of philosophical theology, from Plato to Whitehead, can be focused on the relations between three propositions:
>
> (1) The world is mutable and contingent;
> (2) The ground of its possibility is a being unconditionally and in all respects necessary and immutable;
> (3) The necessary being, God, has ideally complete knowledge of the world.
>
> Aristotle, Spinoza, Socinus, and Process philosophers agree that the three propositions, taken without qualification, form an inconsistent triad, for they imply the contradiction: a wholly non-contingent being has contingent knowledge.[1]

The contrast here is between necessary or noncontingent being and contingent being. Something is "necessary" if it is necessarily the case that it happens or exists; otherwise it is contingent. For example, things that happen by chance are contingent; they don't have to happen, but they happen to happen. Traditionally, God is thought of as a necessary being. As the ground of the possibility of all that exists, God has been thought of as "unconditionally and in all respects necessary and immutable." God does not depend on anything else for existence. But the difficulty that Hartshorne is alluding to is the apparent paradox of how this "wholly non-contingent being has contingent knowledge"; that is, How can God know things that occur by chance? Often this will be stated in terms of future events. Can God know what I will have for breakfast tomorrow morning? I might break from my normal routine and have cereal instead of eggs. How can God know this when it has not happened yet? And if the world changes in time, God's knowledge of the world must also change, which would then mean a change in God.

Many theologians in the process school of thought find their approach to be liberating for Christians who are stuck in a view of God as static and oppressively powerful. Their effort is to free believers from the idea that God has determined a world system from the beginning of time, a system that leaves little room for novelty and creativity, either at the human or the nonhuman levels of creation. Bruce Epperly puts it as follows:

> More than that, process theology presents an open-ended vision of the universe and human life in contrast to many traditional academic and popular theologies, which assert that God determines in eternity every event in our lives. Process theology asserts that God does not and cannot control everything. Rather than being bad news, process theologians believe that the reality of divine limitation opens the door to greater human creativity and responsibility. We have a role as God's companions in healing the planet.[2]

Process philosopher Joseph Bracken pursues this same line of thought in his response to an article by Elizabeth Johnson. Johnson had noted concerns from some thinkers about the difficulty that classical theism has "in moving away from divine determinism to allow for the genuinely random to occur."[3] Bracken suggests that a pure "process" line of thought is actually a more coherent way of dealing with the issue of contingency and necessity. Bracken's focus, however, is not just on the questions of physical chance and necessity, but on the implications that these questions have in terms of human freedom. He introduces a distinction between divine nature and divine personhood in order to ensure that God is not responsible for moral evil. "But in the end the creature, as an . . . independent subject of the act of being, can choose to do what it wants. Hence, the creature, not God as a personal being, is morally responsible for the choices that it makes."[4] Process thought involves a massive shift in our understanding of being, from a traditional emphasis on act, to a focus on potentiality, creativity, and change. In process thinking even God is subject to change and creativity:[5]

> The world order within this scheme is still unfolding even for God. That is, even God cannot know with certitude what the creature will choose until after the creature chooses it. God, in other words, must adjust to what creatures decide and thus inevitably takes risks in dealing with creatures. Does this imply that God is in some sense temporal and subject to change? It would seem that this is the price to be paid for claiming that God is a genuine subject of experience in interaction with creatures rather than an abstract object of thought, the term of a logical inference from contingent effect to transcendent first cause.[6]

Indeed, this is a radical price to pay in order to ensure genuine contingency and freedom in the universe. We are certainly a long way from the transcendent God of classical theism, the impassable, immovable, and eternal cause of all being.

The pattern that emerges in process thought is clear. The need to be able to affirm genuine contingency and chance in the universe appears to be incompatible with the God of classical theism, who is conceived as the first, omnipotent (all-powerful), omniscient (all-knowing), and necessary cause of all that is. The only solution offered is to rework traditional concepts of omnipotence, omniscience, impassibility, and eternity. So, it is argued, something has to give: God is not absolutely omnipotent; God's knowledge is receptive rather than purely creative; God suffers and is subject to time. The transcendent God of classical theism is dead, to be replaced by what process thought calls a *dipolar* view of God, a God who is both contingent and necessary, in a world that is itself both contingent and necessary. Such a God cannot but create, but not to the extent of assuming personal responsibility for all that is. As Whitehead argues, "It is as true to say that God transcends the World, as that the World transcends God. It is as true to say that God creates the World, as that the World creates God."[7] To put it in the simple terms expressed by Cynthia's friend, "God needs us as much as we need God."

THE CLASSICAL ARGUMENT

This dipolar view of God is put forward with such passion and confidence that it might come as a bit of a surprise to discover that the problem these theologians and philosophers pose is not a new one. It is not the result of the discoveries of modern science at all, but it was an issue Thomas Aquinas (1225–1274) already knew in the Middle Ages. Though his formulation might be a little bit different, the issues he considers are basically the same.

Being a thorough student of Aristotle, Aquinas could not but be aware of the issue Hartshorne later raised.[8] Being a devout Christian believer he could not but balk at the type of solution process thinkers offer. Not only did Aquinas hold that God created *ex nihilo* (out of nothing), with no preconditions or constraints, he also held that God's plan for the world was effective. Indeed, these two positions are inextricably linked. Only a God who creates *ex nihilo* can be the provident Lord of history, for otherwise God, too, is subject to the constraints imposed by the contingency of creation. How then did he avoid the apparent dilemma these modern critics of classical theism pose?

In the *Summa contra Gentiles* (hereafter SCG), Aquinas deals with questions concerning divine providence and its relation to contingency and necessity.[9] The objections raised by modern authors are already in evidence. "If all things that are done here below, even contingent events, are subject to divine providence, then, seemingly, either providence cannot be certain, or else all things happen by necessity" (SCG, 3, c.94.). We could translate this as follows: "If all things that occur in the universe, even chance events, are part of God's will, then, apparently, either God's will is not sovereign or else everything that happens is totally determined." Again, we find the contrast of divine necessity and the contingency of the created order, as highlighted in process thought. But Aquinas does not accept the same conclusion. Within his long and detailed response we find the following illuminating comment: "If God foresees that this event will be, it will happen, just as the second argument suggested. But it will occur in the way that God foresaw that it would be. Now, He foresaw that it would occur contingently. So it follows that, without fail, it will occur contingently and not necessarily" (SCG, 3, c.94). Or, what God wills to happen through the unfolding of chance, will occur through the unfolding of chance.[10]

We need to explore Aquinas's point here in more depth. To do this we need to introduce some distinctions that Aquinas developed in his own response. The most famous of these is the distinction between *primary* and *secondary* causes. *Secondary causes* are the sorts of things we have been talking about in the earlier chapters. Science is concerned with the study of such causes: Why does the earth revolve around the sun? What causes populations to change over time? The answers to such questions revolve around the classical and statistical lawfulness that can be empirically verified. As we have seen, these patterns of lawfulness can combine in creative ways to create schemes of recurrence, cyclic patterns of events that have a certain probability of emergence and of survival. These types of observations and explanations illustrate what is meant by the notion of a secondary cause.

There is a more fundamental form of causation, however, what Aquinas called a *primary cause*. This is not concerned with these various patterns, but with their very existence. We can witness this distinction in the comments of royal astronomer Martin Rees, who notes, "Theorists may, some day, be able to write down fundamental equations governing physical reality. But physics can never explain what 'breathes fire' into the equations, and actualizes them in a real cosmos."[11] This is especially evident in modern physics where there are competing theories for understanding fundamental particles. None of these theories can claim to be "necessarily" true. They must all stand or fall on empirical evidence. But even verified empirical theories can't explain why it all works. Why? This act of "breathing fire" is what Aquinas means by a primary cause. Empirical evidence tells us *that* fire has been breathed in, which then invites the further question, Why has it been breathed in? What is the cause of existence itself? This is the question of God's existence. It is not a scientific question in that it is not about *secondary causes*, but about the cause of being itself, of *primary causation*.

This distinction between primary and secondary causation clarifies the ranges and limitations of the scientific enterprise. Science has full reign in explaining the world around us in terms of how things happen (secondary causes). But science can never explain existence in itself. It presupposes this existence when it appeals to empirical evidence to verify its various theories. At the same time, we can also see how creation science or intelligent-design theories attempt to make God another secondary cause, another explanation for empirical events, without attending to the deeper level of causation that God provides. God is never a "God of the gaps" to be invoked in explaining what science cannot yet explain.[12]

Thus, were one to ask "Did God make it rain today?" the answer would be "yes" and "no." The answer is "no" in that God is not the cause of the rain as a scientific explanation. Rather, there are meteorological factors (low barometric pressure, abundance of humidity, etc.) that are the immediate secondary causes of the rain. The answer is "yes" in that, had God not made creation as it is, these factors could not have coincided to make rain; in fact, there would be nothing at all. God is the primary cause of the rain but not the secondary cause of the rain. God is the primary cause of everything that exists, in all its concreteness and particularity, past, present, and future. God is, in fact, the Creator of all secondary causes.

This distinction between primary and secondary causes allows Aquinas to make a further distinction between two levels of necessity and chance. We have already discussed the difference between classical scientific laws that operate in every case, all other things being equal, and statistical laws that tell us about the frequency of events happening. These two types of lawfulness transpose Aquinas's distinction between necessary and contingent *secondary causes*. Aquinas, for example, would have no problem in acknowledging the statistical nature of chance variation in evolution as an example of contingent secondary causation. Indeed, he would argue that it is such precisely because God has chosen it to be such. God can operate through such secondary contingent causes to create life in all its variations. Similarly, he would understand Newton's law of gravity as a form of necessary secondary causation. If we drop a ball, then there is a certain necessity that it will fall, according to the law of gravity. Newton's law and other such classical laws operate as an "if-then" account of causation. This is why Newton's mechanics gave rise to the determinism evident in Laplace's position, noted in chapter 1. There is a necessity—a regularity and predictability—built into these relationships.

At the level of primary cause, however, there is the necessary existence of God and the nonnecessary or contingent existence of everything else that exists. Here the use of the term *contingent* does not mean "chance" but simply the nonnecessity of *existence*. Creation is contingent in this sense in that it is totally dependent on some other to give it existence. As Rees has observed, science does not explain why anything at all exists. In that sense the whole universe is contingent. Its existence is not self-explanatory. Either that existence is simply a brute fact with no further explanation (as atheists propose), or that existence has its explanation in something whose existence needs no explanation, or is necessary. And this is what all people call God, as Aquinas would say. For Aquinas, there is no necessity that anything other than God actually exists. The universe is created *ex nihilo*, not out of any preexisting matter, and not out of any inbuilt necessity in God's self. The very fact of creation itself is nothing less than gift, a gratuitous act of a loving God. This and this alone guarantees not only divine omniscience and an efficacious providence, but also the unequivocal goodness of the created order.

In sum, God is the only thing existing whose existence is dependent on nothing other than God's self. God's existence and God's self are identical. In contrast, creation is contingent in the broad sense of being utterly dependent for its very existence on something else. Creation *has* existence while God *is* existence. Creation is contingent in a second sense in that the world God created is not totally determined but unfolds as an interaction of necessary secondary causes (classical laws) and contingent secondary causes (chance probabilities). Whatever God might create would be contingent (dependent). As it happens, God created a contingent (in the first sense) world in which contingencies (in the second sense) are operative.

WHAT DOES MODERN SCIENCE ADD TO THE PICTURE? SPACE, TIME, AND MATTER

We have seen that many theologians feel compelled to reconceptualize their understanding of God to accommodate the findings of modern science. The argument above demonstrates that such a shift is not required, because one can accommodate genuine contingency (chance) without abandoning a classical conception of God as transcendent and necessary cause of all that is. With this in mind, let us further refine our critique of these alternate proposals. One way or another, proposals that seek to make God into a changing God embed God in the temporal order. Joseph Bracken is most explicit on this: "Does this imply that God is in some sense temporal and subject to change? It would seem that this is the price to be paid for claiming that God is a genuine subject of experience in interaction with creatures rather than an abstract object of thought, the term of a logical inference from contingent effect to transcendent first cause."[13] All this raises the question of the nature of time. What is time and what would it mean for God to be subject to time? To answer such a question we need to listen to what science tells us about time, just as in dealing with the question of evolution we need to listen to what scientists say about descent with modification in species. The problem is, what science says about time runs against so many of our commonsense expectations that it is easy to get confused and fail to realize the full implications of that science.

Let's begin with our common experience of time. We all know there are twenty-four hours in the day, and we measure the passing of time with clocks and watches that tell us when we should be at work or at class, or when our favorite television show is on. Within this flow of time we have a sense of "now," some fleeting moment behind which everything is past and in front of which everything is future. And so the universe is divided into the past, which was real but is no longer real; the now, which is real; and a future, which is not yet real. This sense of time flowing is "objective" in that instruments measure it independent of our experience. Sometimes our own personal experience of time, "subjective time," is very different from this "objective time." Sometimes our personal sense of time slows down, and time drags, and other times it rushes past and we do not know where the time went.

Still, the notion of "now" is firmly embedded in our consciousness. There are complexities, however. We readily accommodate the fact that people live in different time zones from our own. When someone travels from Sydney to Los Angeles, they have the uncanny experience of arriving before they left, because they cross over the international dateline and gain a day. So our notion of "now" can also take into account our conventions in assigning times and dates to different places around the globe.

If we take this notion of time and imaginatively extend it to the whole universe we basically arrive at the notion of time that underpinned Newton's understanding of time and space. Every point in the universe can be assigned a unique set of numbers that specify its location and its time relative to my "now." In this way my "now" is part of a universal "now" that extends across the whole cosmos. Integrated into Newton's "three laws of motion" and his theory of gravitation, this approach proved remarkably successful in explaining the motion of the moon around the earth and the planets around the sun, and a range of other astronomical phenomena. So successful was this scientific approach that it became a paradigm for what science really is.

The first problems with this approach arose when James Clarke Maxwell (1831–1879) discussed the mathematical equations governing electromagnetic phenomena, including light waves. These equations did not entirely conform to Newtonian expectations. To get around this problem, scientists posited some medium through which light must travel, just as sound travels through air. This medium they called the "luminiferous aether." Various experiments were developed to try to detect this aether, the most famous being the Michelson-Morley experiment (1887), which attempted to detect differences in the speed of light as the earth moved in different directions through the aether. Significantly, they failed to detect any difference in the speed of light whichever direction they sought to measure it. This remained a puzzle until a young patent clerk named Albert Einstein developed his theory of special relativity based on the notion that the speed of light is always a constant independent of any particular observer. This notion revolutionized our understanding of space and time.

Consider our notion of time. Einstein proposed a little thought experiment: imagine you are on a light beam traveling away from a clock. As you move away from the clock, what do you see? Because you are traveling away with the light beams that emanate from the clock, the hands on the clock do not appear to you to move. From your point of view, time at the clock stands still. In a way that he was able to make mathematically precise, Einstein predicted that, from the point of view of a "stationary" observer, time slows down significantly as one approaches the speed of light. While this might confound all our common-sense expectations, this phenomenon has been demonstrated countless times in physics laboratories. For example, many subatomic particles decay over a period of time with a well-measured half-life. When they are accelerated to near the speed of light, however, this half-life can be extended greatly in the time frame of the stationary observer.[14] This means that time flows at different rates for people moving at different speeds relative to one another.

This has profound consequences for our common-sense notion of "now." Suppose we have three persons at points A, B, and C, all traveling relative to one another at different speeds. Suppose A and B decide on a common frame of reference for "now" and B and C do likewise for a common "now." Using Einstein's theory of relativity, one can show that A and C will not have a common understanding of "now" using what A and B have decided upon and what B and C have decided upon. Unlike a Newtonian understanding of space and time where this is one common "now" for the entire universe, on Einstein's understanding of space and time there can be no common "now" for the entire universe. There are only "nows" relative to each observer. For Einstein, space and time are not separable realities, but intimately related to one another. This same relativity of "now" persists in his more developed theory of general relativity.

The interrelation of space and time can be illustrated by some of the pictures that have been sent back to earth by the Hubble Space Telescope. While the pictures appear to us in two dimensions, if we align the stars according to distance from the earth and turn the photos into videos, we see ourselves moving out into space toward the furthest stars. What one needs to grasp is that, in such a journey, we are not only moving *out* into space we are moving *back* in time. The light we see from the furthest stars is the oldest and is taking a long time to get to us. So the light we see from nearer stars is "more recent," while the light further out (in distance) is also "older." In fact, the very notion of "light years" reflects this interrelation between time and distance. We measure space by the time it takes for light to get from one point to another. So a star that is two thousand light years away is a star from which light must travel for two thousand years to reach earth. Distance is measured by time in relation to the speed of light.

To illustrate this relativity of space and time, physicist and popular author Brian Greene asks us to consider the following thought experiment, which is not realizable in practice yet demonstrates the underlying mathematics of relativity. Imagine two locations, one with us here on earth and another some ten billion light years away with some alien creature. Assume no relative motion between them and that we both agree on a mutual "now." Suppose that our distant friend decides to move slightly, walking away from us at a small speed. Then his "now" will consist of events in our past. On the other hand, if he were to move toward us at the same speed, his "now" would include events in our future.[15] This type of thought experiment, whose conclusions arise as a simple consequence of Einstein's theories, imply that there is simply no such thing as "now," no universally acceptable definition of simultaneity. As Greene concludes:

> Past, present, and future certainly appear to be distinct entities. But as Einstein once said, "For we convinced physicists, the distinction between past, present and future is only an illusion, however persistent." The only thing that's real is the whole of spacetime. . . . In this way of thinking, events, regardless of when they happen from any particular perspective, just *are*. They all exist. They eternally occupy their particular point in spacetime.[16]

To emphasize this conclusion he later states, "Under closer scrutiny, the flowing river of time more closely resembles a giant block of ice with every moment forever frozen into place."[17]

This means that we have to be very careful about attempting to put God into the flow of time. If there is no universal "now," what might it mean to say the God knows what is happening "now," but not what is going to happen in the future? Past, present, and future are all relative to particular observers. If we place God into time, into our "now," then we privilege a particular time and make it God's time, something that Einstein's theory of relativity rules out. Far from being more attuned to the notion of an evolving world, the possibility that God, too, exists in a flow of time runs into scientific problems.

The alternative is that God's existence is not caught up in the flow of time. God's existence is timeless, eternal, and unchanging. In fact, this is the conclusion Paul Davies draws: "Time is part of the physical universe, inseparable from space and matter. Any designer/creator of the universe must therefore transcend time, as well as space and matter. That is, God must lie *outside* time if God is to be the designer and creator *of* time."[18] As he goes on to note, this is also exactly the conclusion drawn by Augustine. Time, too, is part of creation, and a God who creates the universe creates not just space and matter, but time as well.

We can push this further by noting the interconnections modern physics makes between space, time, and matter. Einstein's account of special relativity posits not a three-dimensional space but a four-dimensional space-time, thus eliminating a Newtonian notion of absolute space and absolute time. Rather, the intelligibility of space and time are interrelated and relative to observers. Time has no intelligibility apart from space on this account. For example, as we have seen already, the common-sense notion of simultaneity is meaningless in special relativity. For one observer two events might be simultaneous, while for another observer who is moving relative to the first observer, the two events are temporally separate.

Einstein's theory of special relativity remains an idealization, however, since it prescinds from the existence and presence of matter. To overcome this deficiency Einstein developed his theory of general relativity, which incorporated matter and hence gravitational effects into its account of space-time. This elucidated the intrinsic interconnections between space, time, and matter. In this account, the presence of matter deforms both space and time. This deformation is what we call gravity. This theory made some quite different predictions than Newton's theory of gravity, was able to explain observed variations in Mercury's orbit, and predicted the bending of light in gravitational fields. So far this theory has survived a number of such experimental tests.

These interconnections are further reinforced by quantum theory, which demonstrates that even the empty vacuum of space is a seething ocean of virtual particles.[19] The existence of these particles is postulated as a consequence of the Heisenberg Uncertainty Principle. While commonly this is taken to mean we cannot measure both position and velocity simultaneously, the same observation holds for energy and time. These "virtual" particles can emerge for small periods of time as long as the energy of these particles over their lifetime does not violate the uncertainty principle.[20] This phenomenon can be verified in what is called the Casimir effect. In this experiment two parallel uncharged metal plates are placed very close to one another. Their closeness actually forces an alignment of the virtual particles between them, which then exerts a force on the plates themselves. This demonstrates that even in a complete vacuum, space is never "empty." This effect has been measured as quantum theory predicts.[21] From this we can see that space, time, and matter are interconnected and inseparable realities. More recent attempts to unify the perspectives of general relativity and quantum mechanics, so-called "string theory," abandon four-dimensional space-time to work in ten or even eleven dimensions of space-time. Matter is thought of as the harmonics of vibrating space-time, whose dimensions are so tightly curved as to remain undetectable to our grosser senses.[22]

What all this science seems to be saying is that time is unintelligible apart from a scientific understanding of space and matter. This fits neatly with the view of classical theism that time is as much a created reality as space and matter, a position both Augustine and Aquinas articulated. As Augustine notes: "For God also made time, and thus there was no time before he made time. Hence, we cannot say there was a time when God had not yet made anything. For how could there be a time that God had not made since he is the maker of all time? And if time came to be with heaven and earth, there cannot be a time when God had not yet made heaven and earth."[23] There is no "before" creation because there is no measure of time without space and matter. So any attempt to place God within the temporal flow will inevitably implicate God in space as well. If God is temporal, God would also have to have a body—to be "here" or "there." While process thought might accept this as "the price to be paid for claiming that God is a genuine subject of experience in interaction with creatures rather than an abstract object of thought," for many it would be too high a price to pay; it simply does not conform with scientific expectations.

In essence, in order to conceive of God properly, we need to get beyond the common-sense notion that God is just like us only really really really *big* and really really really *old*. This picture thinking makes of God a creature like ourselves who had a beginning, lives in a place out there somewhere, and will have a future. Not only is this God, by definition, not God but a creature, this remains an infantile notion of God in the face of the findings of modern science. God is completely "other than" creation, and the divine mode of existence is completely different from anything we come across in our normal experience.

A POSITIVE ACCOUNT

Before concluding this chapter we would like to present a more positive account of the questions of providence, contingency, and creation, one that draws on some contemporary scientific concerns. Popular science fiction often draws on notions of parallel universes and/or time travel causing the branching of history along alternate paths.[24] Behind these fictional accounts lie two distinct theories found in modern science. The first is the Everett-Wheeler "many worlds" interpretation of quantum mechanics.[25] Here the quantum-wave equation for the universe should be thought of as representing all possible variations of our current universe, all considered equally real. Each time a different quantum event happens in "our" world, we should think of the world branching off into all the other possible quantum outcomes for that event. Still, each of these outcomes operates with the same physical laws as we experience in our current "universe." Each of these worlds is real, though our awareness remains within just one of them.

Second, and more recently, some have proposed a multiverse account of the cosmos, which views the cosmos in terms of causally disconnected "universes," each with very distinct physical laws. For example, in such other "universes" the force of gravity may be different, or the mass of various particles may vary, and so on.[26] In this way all possible universes with all possible sets of coherent physical laws are considered to be real. This has been proposed as a counterargument to those who hold that our universe appears "fine-tuned" for life, implying some type of design argument.[27] On the multiverse account, while it is true that life occurs in our universe, there are countless other universes in which life is simply not possible. Our universe is then just a statistical outcome out of all the various possibilities. In their own ways these two theories give some expression to medieval notions of "all possible worlds." Both the "many-worlds" approach to quantum mechanics and the multiverse theories give expression to mathematically possible worlds. The difficulty with both these theories is that the existence of these other worlds is in principle unverifiable.[28]

How can we relate this to our question of creation, providence, and chance? With perfect intelligence God grasps all possible worlds, with all possible branchings, in all possible "universes," precisely as possibilities, in a single act. With perfect wisdom and love, God chooses one possibility in its totality from its beginning to its final consummation, from all the myriad options presented by divine intelligence, in that same creative act. In Martin Rees's expression, God "breathes fire" into one of the many mathematically possible worlds on offer. And so with complete power God realizes that one possibility, making of it the one universe that exists, the one we inhabit, in all its necessity and contingency, determinisms and chance events, again in a single divine act. God's election of this creation eliminates none of its contingency, because God knows, loves, and creates this universe with precisely this set of contingencies "built in." We do not need to place God in time in order to preserve the contingency of the universe, nor do we need to eliminate a divine and efficacious providence. For God is the answer, not to the contingency of chance events per se but to the much more profound contingency of being. It is the contingency of the very being of the universe that requires a necessary being as its source. Once we grasp this fact of divine transcendence, transcending matter, space, and time, the divine knowledge, love, and creation of the lesser contingency of chance events is implied as an automatic consequence.

In presenting all this there are still large questions that remain unaddressed. The two big questions concern divine providence and how that might work in practice. If God's providence is effective, how do we deal with questions of natural evil (earthquakes, tsunamis, droughts, and so on) that affect human suffering? The other big question is that of moral evil: How do we account for the presence of evil and sin in the world in a way that God is not responsible for them, if providence is indeed so effective? Can such a God still be good? We will take up these difficult questions in chapter 5.

CREATOR GOD, EVOLVING WORLD

CONCLUSION

Let us recap our position. The claim is regularly made that the classical notion of a transcendent God, an immutable and unchanging God, is no longer acceptable to modern scientific notions of the universe. Our existence here is simply the product of a large number of chance events. From this, some atheists conclude that God is no longer needed because chance denies any sense of divine purpose. Others who are believers have concluded that God, too, must change, to accommodate a world of chance and change. What we have shown is that neither of these positions is necessary to accommodate what science is telling us of the universe. The classical understanding of God is more than at home with a world of chance and change. But the claims of those who would place God within the temporal flow are in fact more problematic when viewed against what science is telling us about the nature of space, time, and matter.

This conclusion may come as a surprise to those for whom the notion of a changing God has become something of a theological commonplace. However, it does conform with Christian belief in a God who is unchangingly loving, constantly reliable, unswervingly compassionate, a provident God who has counted the hairs on our head and knows when the smallest sparrow falls to the ground. Such a God is a mystery indeed, and divine existence is beyond anything that we can imagine. But such a God sits more than comfortably with everything modern science is telling us about the universe.

CHAPTER 4

EVOLVING WORLD: PURPOSE AND MEANING

We began chapter 2 with a story about a learned gentleman who believed that the mountains and forests "could not all be an accident." He assumed a contradiction between a world in which chance is operative and a world in which there is design and purpose. We subsequently clarified that chance and necessity, random events and ordered laws, do not cancel one another out. In fact, the world has emerged and continues to function as an interaction between classical laws and statistical laws. In chapter 3 we dealt with the question of God in relation to an emergent world. The key point there was that one need not subject God to chance or change just because one accepts the role of chance in evolution. We can retain the idea of a thoroughly transcendent God, a God not subject to change, while acknowledging real contingency of the world God created.

Throughout these chapters we have been adding nuance to polarities that are assumed in debates over creation and evolution, or religion and science in general. The goal of this chapter is to refine our notion of purpose in the universe. Embedded in the false opposition of chance and necessity is the presumption that a world in which chance is operative will necessarily be a world that is directionless, meaningless, and without purpose. Here we argue that the directionality that is thus discredited is tied to a mechanistic determinism, left over from the era of Newton and his influence. Emergence as an interaction of regularity and probability leaves room for an orientation built in to the world's unfolding. We will explore the notion of "finality" as an upwardly but not determinately directed dynamism. In fact, a paradigm that includes a natural orientation toward complexity is gaining ground in recent empirical and theoretical scientific work.

TELEOLOGY AND DARWINISM

The world in which Darwin lived embodied a strong sense of teleology, the notion that everything has its assigned place in the world, and that each thing is ordered to its distinctive "end" or "telos."[1] Newton's discoveries and his new methodological and mathematical way of exploring and explaining the world saturated all kinds of inquiry in the eighteenth century. Indeed, its influence spread to religious views of God and of creation. The eighteenth-century God of Deism, who created the planets and the laws of motion by which they turn, also had created each species in its assigned niche. William Paley (1743–1805) was a vicar and theologian whose defense of such a God dominated the nineteenth century. His 1802 publication *Natural Theology, or Evidences of the Existence and Attributes of the Deity*[2] influenced Darwin's early education. It was against this view of the world with its deterministic teleology that Darwin's theory of natural selection would butt heads.

Paley and those like him ascribed to a view of creation in which God had created each species to fit nicely in the corner of the world it inhabited. Paley used an analogy common in his day: if one were to go out for a walk and find a watch lying on the ground, one would presume that there was a watchmaker who had crafted this artifact. Thus one could conclude not only that there is a Creator but that each piece of the universe is like a crucial mechanical device, each playing its role so that the intended whole will operate according to design. This is generally understood as the theory of special creation.

Darwin, of course, was not the first to challenge such a worldview.[3] The newly unfolding science of geology first opened the door to questioning the age of the earth and introduced the idea that even rocks might morph over time.[4] Furthermore, others, such as Jean-Baptiste Lamarck (1744–1829), had suggested that organisms develop from one generation to another, passing their biological improvements on to later generations. So even before Darwin the notion of a dynamic creation in which entities would shift their structures over time had already presented itself, challenging the idea that creation and biological species were the same forever and for always.

These challenges did not mean that a purpose-driven worldview was immediately eliminated. Rather, the nineteenth century saw a host of ways in which scholars attempted to reconcile a dynamically changing world with mechanisms driving such a world toward certain ends. A few examples will suffice to illustrate the tensions and alternatives as the orderly and stable world of Newtonian laws began to give way to an ever-changing creation, driven, at least in part, by chance events.

Initially, there were the traditionalists trying to hold on to the notion of a stable and orderly, unchanging world. This view is represented not only by William Paley as a theologian but by George Cuvier (1769–1832), one of the curators of the French Museum of Natural History in Paris at the end of the eighteenth century.[5] In general, Cuvier, and then Richard Owen (1804–1892) in the next generation, accepted that there were a number of lineages in living organisms (*embranchements* in French). Nevertheless they insisted on the impassibility of such *embranchements*. They accepted a Platonic "typological essentialism." Adaptation of organisms to their niches might take place within these established branches, but morphing from one branch to another was an unacceptable theorem.

As already mentioned, Lamarck, a co-worker of Cuvier's at the French Museum of Natural History, took a very different view. He insisted that the *embranchements* of natural kinds could indeed be crossed.[6] But this did not necessarily involve adopting a worldview in which meaningless chance events drive the unfolding of earthly life. Though a materialist and atheist who had strident anticlerical sentiments, Lamarck had a very strong notion of progress in the unfolding of life's endeavors. Instead of design by an external Creator, Lamarck believed that there was an inherent tendency among living things to move toward higher and higher life forms, ending with human life.[7] Thus the father of evolutionary theory held a strong sense of automatic progress among and between species over time.

As the debates and dramas over a growing understanding of a dynamic biological history unfolded in the nineteenth century, the notion of design or direction was not as much jettisoned as it was refined. By the mid-1800s the dynamism of the natural world was taken for granted, and the field of embryology was making great advances. One of the greatest embryologists, Karl Ernst von Baer (1792–1876), subscribed to an epigenetic view of embryo development whereby embryos move from more generic processes to ever more differentiated states,[8] driven by "vital forces." *Vitalism* insisted that living organisms had forces at work that could not be reduced to material, physical processes. It supported arguments against the "transmutation" of species. The theory was that the true endpoint of organismic development occurs when an organism reaches reproductive maturity, at which point the vital forces would spin themselves out, leaving nothing to generate moves across the species barrier. The point is that the neoclassical biology of the nineteenth century could incorporate dynamism while clinging to a teleology of fixed species.

What about Charles Darwin? Where did his theory of natural selection fit within the panoply of worldviews available to him? In fact, Darwin shared with Owen and von Baer an epigenetic view of organismic development. But he rejected any typological essentialism that would fix species as unchanging. In this he would accept Lamarck's claim about the possibility of the transmutation of species. But his views rejected both Lamarck's optimism in the progress of species development and the vitalism of von Baer and Owen.

Darwin was driven to ask bigger questions about the effects of environments on species and, hence, on their legacy over time. On his voyage around the world on the HMS Beagle, Darwin realized that there was not a clear correspondence between habitats and species. He visited the Cape Verde Islands, off the west coast of Africa. He then visited the Galapagos Islands, off the west coast of South America. Both sets of islands were similar in longitude and latitude and environment. But Darwin discovered that the flora and fauna of the Galapagos were closer to species found on the mainland of South America than they were to those in the Cape Verde Islands. Apparently, environmental niches did not necessarily come with corresponding species. If special creation were true, had God make a mistake?

What was distinctive about Darwin's revolutionary insight was that he sought an explanation of the connection between species and their environments, and between species themselves, in external forces.[9] Rather than God creating fixed species for given habitats, or the march of progress, or some inner vital force, Darwin concluded that forces outside the organism could, over time, change species.

What Darwin needed was twofold: (1) a theory of inheritance by which traits are passed down from one generation to the next; and (2) an explanation of how environmental forces effect changes in populations over time. Being a good Newtonian, he expected the latter to be a classical law, like the law of gravity only operative in living organisms.[10]

The first element, a mechanism for inheritance by which traits perdure over time, left Darwin in the realm of speculation. He posited that there are little "granules" or "gemmules" that carry reproductive information.[11] The second piece, the discovery of a law by which organisms adapt to environments, became the centerpiece of Darwin's innovations. It came to him via two sources. First there was the well-documented insight that Darwin had in reading Thomas Malthus's (1766–1834) *An Essay on the Principle of Population.*[12] Malthus had posed the question of why, when populations increase in geometrical proportions over time, the world does not become overpopulated in short order. His answer lay in the scarcity of resources. The limitation of available food, shelter, and habitat serve as a mechanism to rein in exponential growth. In every generation there are those who die off because they are unable to compete for limited assets. Darwin was captivated by this "struggle for existence." He took it one step further in realizing that "under these circumstances favorable variations would tend to be preserved, and unfavorable ones to be destroyed. The result of this would be the formation of a new species. Here I had at last got a theory by which to work."[13]

The second clue came to Darwin from his experience with animal breeders. Darwin noted that humans could take dogs or pigeons or cows or pigs, and, by controlling who mates with whom, create specimens that exhibit highly desirable characteristics. These could have to do with milk production or more aesthetic qualities in the feathers of pigeons. The key was that reproduction practices can and have been used by humans to orient the direction nature takes as generations unfold. If this is *artificial* selection, why not consider *natural* selection? Might not nature herself, through the competition for resources, eliminate those with the least ability to survive, leaving the more adapted organisms and species to reproduce?[14]

The key point is that Darwin did not set out to use chance to destroy the teleological determinism of special creation. In fact, he thought he was discovering a law like the law of gravity that would explain a mechanism by which organisms and species over long periods of time could change. The revolutionary part of his theory, what gave such pause to his contemporaries, was twofold. He attributed changes to external natural forces rather than to any internal unwinding of preset forms. Further, his theory did not set any limits or boundaries to the work of these external forces. Whereas others accepted adaptation within the limits of certain body plans or for nonhuman species only, Darwin felt that this law of natural selection applied to all living beings.[15]

These contentions, set over against a teleology that specified particular ends for natural forces, upset an entire worldview. The typological essentialism of his day made Darwin's open-ended natural forces seem capricious at best.

This capriciousness of natural selection clearly challenged the religious views of Darwin's day.[16] Those who wanted to stand up to the clerical upper classes clung to the fact that natural selection seemed to rule out any divinely established hierarchy, enforcing their political claims in favor of democracy. Surprisingly, however, even the antireligious forces of the late nineteenth century included a notion of progress in their theories of evolution. Though Darwin had strenuously tried to distance himself from such ideas, his work and his name were adopted in support of old evolutionary ideas that still incorporated a version of preestablished ends toward which evolutionary process was headed.[17] David Depew and Bruce Weber summarize the issues at the end of the nineteenth century as follows:

> As a result, the main issue now became whether directional evolution should be envisioned in materialistic, humanistic, and anticlerical terms, as Haeckel and Darwin's French translator, for example, hoped; or as a spiritual process in which, in an evolutionary reinterpretation of the old Romantic idealism, the divine comes to consciousness of itself in and through evolutionary progress, as some liberal Protestants, especially in America, came to believe.[18]

Evolutionary theory and Darwinism have taken a number of dramatic turns since this point at the end of the nineteenth century. The rise of modern genetics along with advances in statistical method led to what came to be known as the *modern synthesis* of evolutionary theory in the 1940s and 1950s.[19] The unpacking of the structure of DNA as the basis of inheritance in 1953 began yet another wave of research incorporating molecular biology.[20] We cannot review all these fascinating twists and turns in the evolution of Darwinism. We will mention, however, two further acts in this drama since they are relevant to what we have to say later in the chapter.

First, what was known as "developmentalism" at the turn of the twentieth century is of interest due to recent work in embryology. The position was that phylogeny—the unfolding of species—should be viewed as an inner driven process like the unfolding of an embryo: ontogeny. Specifically, a theory known as *recapitulationism* held the day.[21] This was the view that each embryo moves through all the stages of life's evolution before it settles at its particular species plateau. The diagram of the tree of life (fig. 4.1) created by Ernst Haeckel (1834–1919) shows this clearly—it is an old gnarled tree with many branches, but one solid and clearly emerging trunk that leads up through the levels of life (from amoeba to invertebrates to vertebrates) to reach its climax at MAN.[22] Thus phylogeny drove ontogeny, both of which followed an automatic process timed to unfold like clockwork.[23]

FIGURE 4.1: "PEDIGREE OF MAN" FROM ERNST HAECKEL[24]

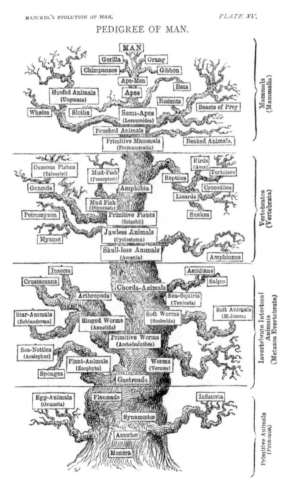

This approach is understandable since the most obvious example of natural forces unfolding toward a telos lies in individual development—acorns become oak trees, tadpoles become frogs, eggs become chickens, and fetuses become human infants. Nevertheless, a residual determinism in this approach proved fatal with the ascendency of natural selection. Its role in species evolution adds an element of contingency that ultimately makes it unlike the programmed order of developmentalist biology. As we will see, however, embryology is now playing a new and essential role in our understanding of evolution and a "new developmentalism" is afoot.

Second, the end of the nineteenth century saw what has been called the "probability revolution." This designates a sea change in scientific method and worldview that took place between the 1840s and the 1920s. This revolution was the result of two trends. The first was the attempt of governments, going back to the 1600s, to keep track of their populace. Initially related to keeping track of deaths due to the Black Plague, record keeping burgeoned with the postrevolutionary governments of the early 1800s. Births, deaths, divorces, political alliances—all were counted in an effort to establish stable states and control subversive elements.[25] At the same time, the mathematical field of probabilities had emerged in an effort to calculate the best course of action when future outcomes were unknown. Scholars sought to quantify how past successes or failures could predict future performance—for example, in a shipping business. When the flood of numbers from the statistical explosion hit this new wave of probability theory, a revolution ensued. Physicists such as J. C. Maxwell (1831–1879) and especially Ludwig Boltzman (1844–1906) began applying such probability thinking to thermodynamics. Eventually, combined with the newly rediscovered genetic work of Gregor Mendel (1822–1884), Darwinism moved to a new level.[26] No longer were contingencies a matter of unexplained phenomena. They could be counted, calculated, and understood as basic to scientific explanation itself.

It is in the wake of this revolution that evolution truly became a science incorporating chance. What followed in its wake were the metaphysical conclusions that world process was about nothing but contingencies. The probability revolution, combined with the horrors of World War I, put all cultural confidence in automatic progress to rest. By the middle of the twentieth century, Paley's watchmaker had been scientifically discredited as blind, and Jacques Monod could claim, "Man at last knows he is alone in the unfeeling immensity of the universe, out of which he has emerged only by chance."[27]

This history of ideas reveals four important points in regard to teleology and Darwinism. First, Darwin's theory of natural selection, while challenging to then current philosophical thinking, did not directly usher in a worldview of chance without any direction. Second, it was part of a much broader shift from a stable world of classical laws to a more dynamic view of the created order as continually changing over long periods of time. Such a shift in thinking most often revised rather than rejected teleology. Third, it is clear that every theory of evolution needs to account for what drives change forward. Even if it is natural selection alone, which operates according to "blind" forces, one must explain both the mechanism of movement and account for the orderliness that emerges. Fourth, scientific theories necessarily incorporate metaphysical assumptions about the nature of the world. These broad philosophical assumptions have an impact on the scientific paradigms at work in empirical research. We thus turn our attention briefly to the interaction of theoretical worldviews and the scientific endeavor.

WORLDVIEWS AND SCIENTIFIC DISCOVERIES INTERTWINED

In general, efforts to understand the world systematically move forward in two dimensions at once. On the one hand, there is the observation of phenomena and the subsequent classification of these, on the premise that similars are to be understood similarly. With the development of refined technologies observation now goes well beyond visual attention; while the simple look into a microscope has not been trumped altogether, much data these days is the product of highly sophisticated technologies and measurements that do not involve just looking.

On the other hand, such on-the-ground empirical work always takes place within a framework of theoretical expectation. Lonergan invokes the metaphor of scissors; scientific investigation involves a back-and-forth movement from the theoretical "upper blade" to the "lower blade" of concrete findings in the here and now. Empirical data—the lower blade—can confirm or challenge the overarching theoretical expectations. At the same time, the model or framework set by the upper blade can guide the experiments or observations pursued by empirical information gathering. Lonergan puts it as follows: "The upper blade, then, is a set of generalities demanding specific determination, and such determination comes from the lower blade of working hypotheses, precise measurements, empirical correlations, deductions of their implications, experiments to test the deduced conclusions, revisions of the hypothesis, and so on, de capo."[28]

Examples through history illustrate the ways in which upper-blade theories can shift entire research paradigms. While most of us are familiar with the Copernican revolution of the sixteenth century, when an earth-centered universe was replaced by a heliocentric system, few realize the important strides Johannes Kepler (1571–1630) made in the following century. As astronomers, mathematicians, and philosophers gradually came to accept the evidence that planets circle the sun, one piece of evidence simply did not meet the anticipated findings. Scientists presumed that the planets orbit the sun in a circular manner, but the orbits as measured did not comply with this expectation. Kepler was able to preserve the heliocentric core of Copernican thinking by dispensing with the assumption that the planets go around the sun in perfect circles. He proposed that the orbits instead take elliptical trajectories. This alternative perspective (upper blade) paved the way for Newton a generation later to explain the gravitational pull that yields such elliptical orbits.

Another example comes from the field of chemistry. Before Dmitri Mendeleev (1834–1907) developed the periodic table, the work of chemists consisted of noting relations between different chemicals and their constituent elements, and the classification of those elements through the similarities of their chemical properties. Still, what was required was a theoretical construct that made sense of these relationships. Was there an underlying pattern to be found? Mendeleev proposed an ordering system based on the notion of an atomic number. This number corresponded to the whole number of protons in the nucleus of the atom of the element. This notion of an atomic number provided an ordering principle for relating the elements to one another in a simple sequence. Soon it was found that there were gaps in the ordering, that is, elements that should be in the sequence of atomic numbers, but had not yet been discovered. In this way the upper-blade ordering principle of atomic number led to the prediction of new elements not then known, gaps in the lower blade of empirical data that were later revealed.[29]

One more recent example of the relationship between upper and lower blades has to do with subatomic particles. These particles are created by large atom-smashing particle accelerators when beams of atoms (or protons and neutrons) are brought to high speeds (near the speed of light) and then bombard one another. The array of debris that emerges from such experiments is then classified according to various properties such as mass, electric charge, spin, and so on. When so classified, scientists identify certain patterns in the data and ask whether these patterns correspond to some underlying intelligibility. Various attempts have been made to provide a theoretical framework for the data gathered, the most successful being what is called the "standard model."[30] This theory views the different particles as variations on an underlying pattern, according to which particles can be transformed into one another by various symmetry operations (somewhat like reflections in a mirror).

This theory (upper blade) has been remarkably successful in bringing theoretical order to the array of experimental data (lower blade). It has also predicted the existence of new particles not originally known, but that subsequently have been discovered, except until very recently for one. This is the famous Higgs boson. This particle was sought in experiments conducted in the Large Hadron Collider, the largest scientific instrument ever constructed, near Geneva, Switzerland. In June, 2012, scientists announced that they seem to have found empirical evidence for the Higgs boson. If they are correct, it will be an important verification for the standard model. If they are not, it will leave the status of the model under a cloud.[31]

These are all examples of the way in which theoretical expectations drive empirical research, and vice versa. But there is a broader cultural dimension to this interaction. Cultural frameworks set limits on what can be considered acceptable science. Thus, not only do scientific understandings of phenomena in the world change, new science can challenge an entire cultural milieu. Likewise, new cultural horizons can allow previously rejected hypotheses to garner new attention.[32]

Thus, for example, Kepler's appeal to elliptical orbits to explain planetary trajectories constituted much more than new calculations of old data. For millennia the circular motions of the heavens, as a particular view of perfection, had been invoked to explain how and why the world worked the way it did. Now, not only had the earth lost its place at the center of the universe, this circularity at the heart of common cultural conceptions of the created order was at stake. In discussing the depth of cultural change incited by these paradigm shifts, Depew and Weber speak of "a deep shift in the sensibility of a whole culture" and then refer to Kepler's innovation: "Belief in the magical superiority of circular movement is a case in point. That is what Kepler had to surrender."[33]

Let us return, then, to Darwin's place in the nineteenth century. Here again, a major shift in both research traditions and cultural assumptions was taking place. In sum, it was the shift from the mechanistic determinism of Isaac Newton and William Paley, in which the laws that drive the world are fixed and deterministic, to a world seen as a dynamic interchange of order and novelty. Chance came to be understood as a key player in this flexible unfolding, but Darwin himself only glimpsed its role indirectly. The recognition of chance, and its taming, as Ian Hacking has named it,[34] would come with the turn to the twentieth century along with the turn to genetics, and then to molecular biology. The notion that world order was nonetheless unfolding toward specified ends has had a tenacity that has perdured in this cultural shift. Unfortunately, such teleology still clings to a deterministic view of world process, whether defending or rejecting a religious ground for world order.

We are still caught in this paradigm shift, from a determined order set in motion way back when, toward a view of the world in which true novelty and uniqueness has a place. Dynamism, fluidity, and constant flux are all now taken for granted in our modern and postmodern worldviews. The question is whether teleology as a directedness embedded in reality is still a viable concept. Can we conceive of the world as both open ended yet in some way directed? If Darwinism in its various forms has challenged the static world that predated it, is there an upper blade that is appropriate to the new cultural milieu of evolutionary science?

FINALITY: A NEW WAY OF CONCEIVING DIRECTIONALITY

What we are looking for is an explanatory framework in which to understand the dynamism of world process as it unfolds. In a very general sense, how can we explain what drives evolution forward? Is it mere chance that enervates evolutionary processes but without any direction? Is it some implanted or imprinted design that unfolds according to a preset plan? We have rejected both of these alternatives as based on faulty understandings of how chance operates as well as on a poor theology of God. How, then, can we conceive of a world process that is dynamic, is directed in some way though open ended, and includes elements of both order and uncertainty? We will present here Bernard Lonergan's notion of *finality* as meeting these requirements.[35]

A preliminary note is necessary. Finality, as a notion of how development unfolds over time is a *heuristic* notion. "Heuristic" comes from the Greek word *heuriskein*, meaning "to discover" or "to find." A heuristic device is an aid to discovery. We can set out clues about what we expect to find before we find it. As such, this does not immediately tell us what the answers to our questions will be, only what elements are likely to be involved once we know these answers. In this same way, finality is a notion, a set of clues, rather than an answer. Just as in algebra we can designate "X" to be the unknown—what we are trying to determine—and begin listing what the characteristics of X are, so we can work out the characteristics of finality before we address any particular set of inquiries about things and their relationships in concrete contexts.

So let us begin with a definition of finality and attend to its various characteristics. Finality is "the upwardly but indeterminately directed dynamism" of world process.[36] This may sound like a jumble of jargon, so let us unpack the meaning of this phrase, one element at a time.

First, the world's unfolding is *dynamic*. To say this is to deny that the world is inert, stable, complete. It is to affirm that the universe is on the move. This recognition is what has been gained in the last two centuries, beginning with a geology that discovered that even rocks are changing, leading up to and including our current understanding of subatomic particles. This is not to deny that there are stable relationships with settled routines on which we can rely. But it is to recognize that even this stability is dependent on dynamic interactions at other levels (for example, chemical reactions depend on electronically charged atoms). It also recognizes that even stable relations can be altered by changing environments.

Second, finality asserts not only dynamism but a *directed* dynamism. This is not to minimize such things as entropy, cataclysm, death, and extinction. Nor is it to insist on some kind of automatic progress. Rather, it points to the fact that relations in the world tend toward greater systematization. Subatomic particles exist in a tension that orients them to the order that emerges in the atom. Atoms exist in a dynamic field that orients them toward molecular bonding. And so on, up through organic chemistry, to sentient life, and then intelligent life. Thus the dynamism is "upwardly directed" in that it heads toward higher integrations. What exactly will emerge in any given situation is unknown until it actually emerges. What exactly emerges depends not on some predetermined plan but on the contingent conditions that happen to exist in any given place and time.

In other words, third, this dynamism is *indeterminately* directed. Though the world and its many complex relations and co-relations are many systems on the move, what will emerge next is not determined a priori. There can be probabilities that one thing rather than another will unfold. We can and do attend to these likelihoods. But as probabilities always include exceptions, and ideal frequencies do not determine actual frequencies, what exactly occurs is known only once it has occurred.

This idea that dynamism might be directed but indeterminate is a difficult one to grasp. Generally, we assume that "directed" means toward a specific product. Likewise, we think "indeterminate" means "without direction." It is worth pausing here to explore how such direction without determination works.

The best example of such dynamism is, in fact, our own native curiosity. If we are interrupted by a beeping sound while reading this text, we immediately try to make sense of it: Is it a fire alarm? My cell phone? A garbage truck outside, backing up? This native curiosity emerges spontaneously. It has an orientation—toward making sense of my experience. But the orientation, while directed, does not in itself answer the question. For this we need more information: Is there smoke in the air? Are others making moves to leave the building? Is there a dumpster outside the building? Did I even bring my cell phone with me?

Eventually, we will gather enough evidence to narrow down the possible explanations. There does indeed seem to be either a fire or a fire drill going on in the building. Note that, in this determination, we have moved beyond just seeking intelligibility—making sense of basic sensory experience. We are now seeking to make a correct judgment. This drive to understand correctly pushes us to figure out which is the best explanation. Once we are satisfied that the sound of running, the fire trucks outside, and the continued loud beeping in the hallway confirm that the sound is a fire alarm, our drive to know the truth comes to a conclusion.[37]

Once we make such a determination, we move to questions for action: What should we do? Several alternative courses of action present themselves: stay put until someone urges us to move, head for the nearest staircase and leave the building, or climb out a window onto the nearest roof. The point is that a natural urge to wonder, "What is the best thing to do in this situation?," exists prior to any answer we give.

This exercise in imaginary queries illustrates a dynamism operative in the world, in this case in our own spontaneous awareness, that is both directed but indeterminate. The orientation of wonder drives us to make sense (seeking intelligibility), to make correct sense (pursuing truth), and to do the right thing (in search of value). Our native intelligence is directed toward intelligibility, truth, and value. But such an orientation is an indeterminate orientation. The determination comes in the concrete, with the asking and answering of specific questions.

There are parallels in the nonhuman world. Atoms with their charged electrons can exist on their own, yet the electrical charges push the basic elements to match up with other atoms to form molecules. Which molecules form is not determined a priori by an external agent, but depends on the proximity and attraction of various atoms to one another. Likewise, simple molecules bond together to form more complex compounds. Which compounds form depends on the molecules available in a particular place and time. Some compounds bond together in such a way that living matter emerges and the interactions that ground organic chemistry, the chemistry of cell metabolism, for example, are established.

The point here is to recognize that built into the dynamism of the world is an orientation toward greater system, from atoms to human wonder. But this orientation is open ended. There is no antecedent agent or blueprint that establishes that these atoms will form these molecular bonds in this time and place. The orientation of finality—this directed dynamism—depends on the concrete circumstances in which certain atoms happen to be in proximity to other atoms with opposite charges. The native wonder of human consciousness generates questions for understanding, truth, and action, but which questions are asked and answered depends on the circumstances in which data that require explanation happen to be experienced.

Let us return to an idea introduced in chapter 2 to explore further this idea of finality. Recall our discussion of a scheme of recurrence. A scheme of recurrence is simply a series of events that are ordered in such a way that the series of events is repeated indefinitely—it recurs. Thus the "upwardly but indeterminately directed dynamism" we have been illustrating has stability points along the way. The internal dynamism of an atom consists of schemes of recurrence in energy exchanges, making atoms both stable and in flux. Chemical compounds are themselves recurrent sets of interactions at the atomic level. Some chemical compounds can react with one another in a series that repeats itself. While these chemical schemes of recurrence are not common in nonliving situations, they are the hallmark of living entities. The Krebs cycle often chemical reactions, recurrent and self-sustaining in every living cell, is but one example of the multiple schemes of recurrence buried in the biochemical processes of a living cell. And we are becoming increasingly aware of the complex schemes of recurrence at work in our natural environment. A habitat is a set of schemes of recurrence that make possible the flourishing of various kinds of life. Destruction of such habitats undercuts the life that they sustain.

The fact that schemes of recurrence occur, and that they occur at multiple levels of organization in the world, reveals the existence of higher integrations of underlying elements. Higher integrations systematize recurrent schemes of lower processes that are otherwise merely coincidental to one another. They are at once dependent on these lower sets of events yet form something altogether different. And so, when neurological processes break down, a person can no longer think straight. Plant life ceases to exist when the chemistry of photosynthesis fails. Still, the human mind is more than and other than neurological processes. Likewise, plant life, while utterly dependent on chemical processes, is a new differentiation that integrates yet goes beyond mere underlying chemical reactions.

We have thus come to the "upwardly" aspect of the notion of finality. Surely, the modifiers "upwardly" and "higher" are used metaphorically. Nevertheless, they point to the reality just indicated—that more complex sets of schemes of recurrence form integrations that are both more than yet dependent upon underlying systems. So we can distinguish between emergence and mere change. Something new emerges when existing realities are integrated into a new system that manifests genuinely new properties, not reducible to the sum of its parts. We can find examples of this in evolution when single-cell organisms joined together to form multicell organisms with internally differentiated structures. We get some insight into this process in the life cycle of the *Dictyostelium discoideum*, a single-cell slime mold.[38] Under certain conditions (probability of emergence), when its food supply is failing, these single-cell organisms will clump together to form a "slug." This slug has a definite front end and back end, it responds to light and temperature gradients, and will migrate to find new food sources.[39] On arrival, the slug differentiates into a base, stalk, and apex containing spores that then disperse into the new environment to return to the state of single-cell organisms. The slug has emerged from its individual constituents and is distinct from them. Once the conditions that necessitated this emergence change, it can return to its underlying elements.

Here we begin to see the importance of probabilities within this world-view. Probabilities, recall, are a measure of the likelihood of some event or series of events occurring—whether batting averages, birth rates, or bush fires. With regard to evolution, probabilities can make sense of both the emergence of new species or variations and the decline or extinction of species or variations. Higher integrations of lower manifolds of events—more complex schemes of recurrence—are subject to both the probabilities of emergence and the probabilities of survival. This accounts for various degrees of stability in the systems that exist. Some schemes of recurrence are highly likely to emerge while fleeting in their existence (have a low probability of survival). This can be true at the atomic level, in terms of chemical compounds, in plant life, animal life, or human knowing. Alternatively, some systems, for example some types of plants, emerge rarely but once they exist are hard to eradicate.[40] These probabilities get even more complicated as one deals with more and more complex schemes and series of schemes of recurrence. Higher schemes of recurrence are always conditioned by the lower sets of processes on which they are based. Hence the probabilities of these lower systems, of their emergence and survival, affect the probabilities of higher systems as well. Furthermore, while some schemes of recurrence develop great stability—with a very high likelihood of survival—such systems lock their underlying manifolds into place so that little innovation can occur. Ironically, it is those schemes of recurrence that are most fragile, subject to fluctuation and breakdown, that yield the most potential for further development.[41]

We should note that it is also possible for the higher-order scheme to modify the behavior of the lower-order system, significantly altering its probability of survival. One example of this is the scheme of recurrence we call the neutron. Particle physicists talk of the neutron as consisting of three quarks constantly exchanging particles that mediate the strong force binding them together. On the one hand, this scheme of recurrence has a finite probability of survival, with a half-life of around eleven minutes.[42] On the other hand, when the neutron is incorporated into the nucleus of an atom like carbon or oxygen, its probability of survival significantly increases.[43] If it did not, none of our basic elements would be stable and life would not be possible.

Note that the drive toward system, and its indeterminacy, is as much apparent in breakdowns and failures as in stability and progress. Indeed, the breakdown of some systems can become the possibility for other things to emerge.[44] Finality does not imply automatic progress by any means. Nor does the world exhibit such determined progress. Rather, what emerges and survives—species, habitats, human cultures—does so according to schedules of probability, both the probabilities of emergence and the probabilities of survival. Finality is thus not a simple-minded formula but reveals a nuanced set of interactions that reflect the multitudinous differentiations of schemes of recurrence over time and place.[45]

Finally, finality as the upwardly but indeterminately directed dynamism of the world's unfolding embodies a great degree of flexibility. When one trajectory of development is derailed, other compensations occur. So, for example, embryonic sea urchins who suffer disruption in early cell division manage to compensate at later stages of development to become normal adults.[46] Examples of such adjustments, compensations, and corrections abound in animal and plant life as well as in environmental milieu. And, in addition to this minor flexibility, there is of course the major flexibility in which new coincidental manifolds at one level provide the materials for a new species or new genera to emerge, as when the fins of aquatic animals adjusted to become the limbs of land animals.

We have been defining and illustrating a general notion of the way in which world process unfolds, whether at the subatomic level or in the case of human wonder. As a heuristic notion, finality serves as an explanatory framework within which specific phenomena and their emergence or decline can be understood. Note, however, that this notion, while abstracting from the concrete investigations of physics, chemistry, biochemistry, botany, or psychology, is not a contrivance added to make theories work out the way we want. Rather, it is an explanation of the way the universe in fact works. While no one specific empirical study will confirm finality as operative, in fact every investigation will implicitly illustrate that there is in the world a dynamism that drives emergence, that this dynamism is directed toward ever-greater systematization and integration, but that the particular integrations that emerge are not determined a priori.

CONVERGENCE: SCIENTIFIC ENDEAVORS ENDORSE DYNAMIC PURPOSE

We have been outlining a framework for understanding evolution with direction in a way that is quite different from random chance as well as from the deterministic design perspective. In fact, recent developments in biology confirm this "direction without determinism" framework. The work of Stuart Kauffman in complexity theory, the projects of Sean Carroll in embryology, and the work of paleontologist Simon Conway Morris all suggest that finality as outlined above is in line with recent empirical and theoretical work.

Kauffman, trained as both a medical doctor and a research biologist, is best known for his work at the Santa Fe Institute—a think tank devoted to theoretical work on complexity theory.[47] He and his colleagues have used computer programs to simulate the unfolding of systems of nature that are dynamic, unpredictable, and fundamentally complex. Complex systems are not merely complicated—a snowflake is complicated but it remains unchanged until it melts. Alternatively, a turbulent river is constantly changing but it changes chaotically. Complex systems lie somewhere in between, as Depew and Weber note: "So identified, complex systems are systems that have a large number of components that can interact simultaneously in a sufficiently rich number of parallel ways so that the system shows spontaneous self-organization and produces global, emergent structures."[48]

To begin to understand such systems, imagine that you have a number of buttons on the floor, with a number of strings with which to attach them. Take any two buttons and put a string between them. If there are twenty buttons, you will be able to make up to ten connections without reusing a button. After that point, any button you connect will already have a string attaching it to a third button. Gradually, the single connections will begin to make a system of interconnected parts. Once you have more threads than buttons the entire thing becomes a giant network of nodes and connectors. At this point if you pick up one button you will have to pick up all of them.

In general, then, the principle is that there is a *phase transition* (as when water suddenly hits the point where it becomes ice) when the number of connections grows to be more than half the number of nodes. So if we were connecting ten thousand elements, a network would suddenly emerge when there were five thousand or more connections. Now, imagine that the nodes are molecules and that the connectors are chemical reactions. More potential relationships emerge. Molecules A and B can produce AB or BA. BA can in turn react again with B to make BBA. BA could react with A to make BAA, and so on. This gets even more complex when one realizes that there are many organic molecules that can be the basis of and products of reactions but simultaneously serve as catalysts to facilitate still other reactions. Eventually, not only do you have so many connections that a giant network forms, the products of some reactions facilitate others, such that a self-sustaining network emerges. Kauffman summarizes this as follows:

> As the diversity of molecules in our system increases, the ratio of reactions to chemicals, or edges to nodes, becomes ever higher. In other words, the reaction graph has ever more lines connecting the chemical dots. The molecules in the system are themselves candidates to be able to catalyze the reactions by which the molecules themselves are formed. As the ratio of reactions to chemicals increases, the number of reactions that are catalyzed by the molecules in the system increases. When the number of catalyzed reactions is about equal to the number of chemical dots, a giant catalyzed reaction web forms, and a collectively autocatalytic system snaps into place. A living metabolism crystallizes. Life emerges as a phase transition.[49]

What Kauffman calls "collectively autocatalytic systems" is parallel to Lonergan's schemes of recurrence. Kauffman insists that this tendency for connections to kick into wider self-sustaining networks indicates an inherent trend in nature towards self-organization. He calls it "order for free."

Let us examine one more example of this order for free. Genes are strings of nucleotides that code for certain proteins. When a gene goes into gear proteins are produced to do any number of jobs in an organism. But in order for this to happen, the gene needs to be activated, or "expressed." So if we reconceive our connectivity graph to involve genes, each gene would have two states it might be in: "on" or "off." Furthermore, there can be a number of inputs by which one gene is connected to another, such as the other genes that serve as switches either to turn the gene on or to repress its activity. Rather than buttons, let's imagine light bulbs. The light patterns that emerge spontaneously in a system of connected bulbs depend on how many bulbs are in the network and how many inputs are required, in what configuration, to turn on any one bulb.[50] In a setup of one thousand light bulbs, the possible scenarios are astronomical. Still, having run such possibilities through a computer, Kauffman and his colleagues discovered the following. Suppose N equals the number of light bulbs (or genes) and K equals the number of inputs (or connections necessary to turn the bulb/gene "on"). If K is quite low, say K = 1, a network is created but nothing very interesting happens—the network freezes up, doing the same thing over and over again. Alternatively, on the other end of the spectrum, if K = N (the number of inputs equals the number of elements being connected) the system that emerges is massively chaotic. Surprisingly, when K = 2, order arises suddenly and stunningly. Even when N = 100,000 and the possibilities are enormous, when K = 2 the network settles down into a relatively small set (317) of ordered routines.[51]

Thus the human genome, with its 25,000 genes, each of which can be on or off, most with one or two connections to other genomic factors, can settle into a limited number of ordered but relatively fragile patterns. Our genetic systems are thus poised on the "edge of chaos"—ordered but not so fixed as to be nonmalleable. In reference to the extremes of frozen order and utter chaos, Kauffman comments: "Just between, just near this phase transition, just at the edge of chaos, the most complex behaviors can occur—orderly enough to ensure stability, yet full of flexibility and surprise."[52]

Kauffman's work serves as a theoretical upper blade that can aid in directing research on the ground.[53] It is very much in line with our explanation of finality as a property of emergent probability. It is also a counterpoint to the paradigm that has undergirded most twentieth-century evolutionary science. This latter entails the assumption that chance mutations crafted by natural selection (elimination) are the only sources of order in the emergence of life in its diverse forms. Kauffman is proposing that large-scale systems over long periods of time exhibit spontaneous self-organization. This is "order for free"—provided by nature's own processes prior to the role of chance variation or natural selection. Such order is then crafted by natural elimination or altered by chance mutations, migration, or drift. There are still many variables and forces at work to determine what actually has emerged and disappeared in life's history. Self-organization, complexity theory, order for free—these are not the same as deterministic design. Rather, they indicate a dynamism toward order—an upwardly but indeterminately directed dynamism—inherent in world process itself.[54]

Another field of research that has burgeoned in the last two decades involves the cooperative and comparative work of embryology and evolution, or "Evo Devo." Not since the end of the nineteenth century have embryologists and evolutionary scientists had as much to do with each other. Recall the developmentalists who assumed that the straightforward development of embryos—ontogeny—was reflected in a similarly predetermined, step-by-step ladder of descent though the ages—phylogeny. This marriage of two predetermined teleologies fell out of favor as the role of probabilities surfaced as central in evolution. As it turns out, the development that unfolds in embryos is not as straightforward a teleology as we previously assumed, either. At the same time, the secrets of evolution are once again being found in the mysteries of embryo growth.

Sean Carroll, in *Endless Forms Most Beautiful: The New Science of Evo Devo*, confirms many of the theoretical expectations Kauffman proposes.[55] While we cannot explore the many examples of development and evolution explained in this book, a few key features are worth noting.

First, the recent mapping of the human genome (2001) has revealed that among the three billion nucleotide bases that form the human genetic code a small segment form approximately 25,000 genes—the "words" that code for proteins which are responsible for the growth and healthy functioning of a human being.[56] Some surprising discoveries have surfaced. Not only is there a smaller number of genes than predicted, the commonality across species is extensive.[57] Humans and apes have a genome that is close to 99 percent the same, while a counterpart to most of the 25,000 human genes can be identified in mice.[58]

Second, it seems that there is a small subset of genes that control body-plan development in the embryo stages of most animals. Carroll outlines a number of these but labels the whole set "tool-kit genes." It is these that determine body segments, appendages, how and where animals take in nourishment and dispose of waste matter. Everything from forewings, antennae, and legs on fruit flies to wing spots on butterflies and stripes on zebras are thus prescribed. The amazing thing is that the same set of body-building genes is shared so widely among different kinds of animals. This commonality also indicates that these gene sets are quite ancient. The Cambrian explosion that took place 545 to 500 million years ago seems to have set basic body plans in place, which were then modified and refined over time. There is evidence, at least by inference, that many of the prevalent body-plan genes that govern animal development today were in place even prior to this Cambrian explosion.[59]

Thus we have extensive sharing of similar yet ancient tool-kit genes across a wide variety of animal types—from spiders with their spinarets to fish with fins to birds with wings.[60] What then can account for this co-existence of both great similarity and grand diversity? The key seems to be not in the genes themselves as much as in the way they are used. For decades biologists assumed that different morphologies (body designs) indicated entirely different genetic sets. Now it turns out that the differences lie in when and where certain quite common genes are turned on. The key lies in genetic "switches." In other words, in addition to *structural* genes that account for the proteins that make blood or bone cells there are *regulatory* genes. These strings of DNA serve to inhibit or encourage gene expression. The work in embryology has shown that *where* in embryo "geography" and *when* during development a certain gene is activated will determine what it generates. As Carroll puts it:

> The most surprising and crucial feature of genetic switches is their ability to control very fine details of individual tool kit gene action and anatomy. The anatomy of animal bodies is really encoded and built—piece by piece, stripe by stripe, bone by bone—by constellations of switches distributed all over the genome.
>
> . . . And switches are hotspots of evolution—they are the real sources of Kipling's delight—the makers of spots, stripes, bumps, and the like. Part genetic computer, part artist, these fantastic devices translate embryo geography into genetic instructions for making three-dimensional form.[61]

Thus the "new developmentalists" studying embryology in conjunction with evolution, have unearthed concrete examples of the complexity Kauffman and his colleagues had worked out in computational mathematics.[62] A few networks of multiple interactions with regard to body forms seem to have leapt onto the stage early on in life's history. This self-organization, networks of schemes of recurrence, then established a foundation that could be and was refined over millions of years. As natural selection favored those with adaptive innovations, and chance provided slight changes that enabled different switches to turn on or off at different times on different embryonic landscapes, new complex schemes emerged while others went extinct. Evolution has not been just a matter of chance set in order by natural selection, but ordered complexity in conjunction with chance, molded by changing environments shifting adaptive traits, altering probabilities of emergence and survival.

One further example of current scholarship adds to this tapestry. Simon Conway Morris is an evolutionary paleobiologist at the University of Cambridge. He has done extensive work on animals of the Cambrian period.[63] In his most recent work, *Life's Solution: Inevitable Humans in a Lonely Universe,* he contradicts the assumption that if we were to run the tape of life over again something entirely and randomly different would unfold.[64] Instead, he documents extensively the many instances of *convergence* in evolutionary history. Evolutionary convergence is "the recurrent tendency of biological organization to arrive at the same 'solution' to a particular 'need.'"[65] In other words, many times over the course of history the same body parts or traits have emerged independently of one another, that is, without a common heritage. Whereas many paleobiologists are interested in lineages—how one species emerged from another, descent with modification—Morris traces commonalities in evolution that are not related to one another.[66]

Perhaps the most commonly known of such convergences are the many ways in which eyes have developed in a wide range of species. This would include the camera-like eye of the octopus and humans. In fact, Morris indicates that camera-like eyes have evolved independently at least six times. Other examples include the sharp canine teeth of two otherwise very different kinds of wildcats and the forelimbs of the praying mantis and another group of insects known as *Mantispa*. The examples abound, as documented in five detailed chapters on convergences in the properties of sight, smell, echolocation, digging and burrowing, hearing, defense tactics, sentience, brains, and the ability to grasp (hands and digits). In addition, he confirms Kauffman's computational work in discussing convergence at the molecular level; the independent emergence of similar organic molecules over and over again as life has evolved.[67]

While it is impossible here to recount these many examples, Morris concludes from these convergent trends that in organic evolution "there is an underlying structure that imposes limits and delineates probabilities of outcomes."[68] While vitalism and notions of progress have long since fallen out of favor,[69] Morris believes that the natural historical record speaks against the "dominance of contingency," the notion that only chance is responsible for what has emerged in the history of life. This view lies far from a teleological determinism and ascribes deep creative significance to adaptation in ecological niches. Just as Kauffman insists on self-organization at the heart of nature's own processes, so Morris concludes that inherent to the universe's unfolding are *formational capabilities*: "Not only is the Universe strangely fit to purpose, but so, too, as I have argued throughout this book, is life's ability to navigate to its solutions."[70] He finds the following salient facts of evolution to be congruent with creation as a purposeful endeavor: (1) its underlying simplicity, using a few building blocks; (2) its ability to navigate amongst an immense set of possibilities to the minute fraction that work; (3) the sensitivity of the process, in which almost all alternatives are catastrophic; (4) the inherent tendency of life toward the emergence of complexity through the rearrangement and co-option of existing elements; (5) the exuberance of diversity at the same time as the ubiquity of convergence; and (6) the inevitability of the emergence of sentience among a more widely varied group of animals than we generally recognize.[71]

CONCLUSION

We have been outlining a worldview that rejects the old static view of deterministic special creation but nevertheless incorporates a notion of direction in the unfolding of evolution. Finality as a notion of direction without determination not only serves our purposes but can be grounded in the world as it actually operates. Something like finality is affirmed in recent theoretical and empirical work. Thus Depew and Weber finish their long narrative on the history of Darwinism by summing up current thought: "Still, we need not be overly skeptical about evolutionary direction and complexification, or even of teleological process."[72] Later they conclude, in reference to the watchmaker notion of design:

> From our perspective, however, there is no watchmaker, blind or sighted, for the simple reason that there is no watch. Natural organization is not an artifact, or anything like it, but instead a manifestation of the action of energy flows in informed systems poised between order and chaos. Directionalities, propensities, and self-organization in a thermodynamic perspective actually exclude the notion that evolution is oriented toward an end in the intentional or design sense. The thermodynamic perspective allows biological adaptedness precisely by excluding design arguments. Directionality excludes directedness.[73]

Indeed, we have argued for a dynamic teleology without invoking God or God's design at all. It remains now to indicate how this teleological view is coherent with the theism we endorse. That is, how would a teleology of finality make sense of the notion of God's provident will?

CHAPTER 5

HUMAN FREEDOM AND GOD'S PROVIDENCE

Robin Ryan, in the introduction to his book on God and suffering, recounts the story of a couple he calls Mary and John.[1] Mary told him how, six months previously, John had been in a severe car accident. Driving in the dark on a wet and winding road, John had encountered a car coming at him at a high speed. The head-on collision left the other driver injured, though he did survive. John's car was completely demolished but John walked away without a scratch. The policeman who came to the scene was incredulous, even calling John's survival a "miracle." In gratitude that his life was spared, Mary and John told this story over and over in the subsequent months, highlighting the way in which God had saved John's life. Then, three months after John's accident, the teenage daughter of some close friends was killed in a car accident. Mary and John surrounded them with love and walked closely with them through their grief. But Mary and John, while still grateful that John's life had been spared, felt that they could no longer talk about John's escape from harm as a matter of God's protection. If God's providence had been at work in John's accident, what were they to say to their friends—that God had not been provident when their daughter was killed? These are the issues we need to explore in this chapter.

In chapter 3 we considered the relationship between God and creation in terms of the classical understanding of God as a transcendent and necessary cause of all that exists. In particular we noted how an understanding of God as primary cause, or cause of being, gave full scope for science to understand the universe, leaving divine agency at a different level of explanation. We further explored this in terms of God's sovereign election or choice of our world, our universe, from all possible universes, choosing ours to exist, to be, to be real. The act of election is a single act that encompasses the totality of our existence, from the beginnings of the cosmos in the Big Bang, to the final fate of that same cosmos, whatever that fate might be.[2] God's act is outside of time; it is timeless, but it creates space, matter, and time. Further, this stance is fully congruent with the way in which modern science views space and time.

This is, of course, a big claim and it raises some very difficult questions for believer and nonbeliever alike. Mary and John's experience raises questions about whether God is good and, if so, how God seemingly fails to act when tragedies occur. If God chooses this universe, in all its details from beginning to end in a single act, why does God allow there to be suffering and evil? Why does God choose a world in which suffering and evil occur? And is God then not responsible for suffering and evil? Such questions are not abstract ones. When we look at recent human history there have been unimaginable horrors, both humanly created, such as the Holocaust, and naturally occurring, such as recent tsunamis in Asia. At a more personal level, we all know friends and loved ones who have suffered and died from causes both natural and unnatural. Should we lay all these at the feet of God and demand an explanation, like Job railing against God? As we have seen in chapter 3, some of the theologians who have objected to the classical understanding of God have done so precisely in order to absolve God from responsibility for such horrors.

More significantly, for some people these horrors are proof that God simply does not exist. How can an omnipotent and loving God allow suffering and evil to occur? Either God is not omnipotent, unable to eliminate them, or God is not loving, unwilling to eliminate them. The Christian God is then viewed as internally contradictory and hence nonexistent. This is a common, and some find powerful, atheist objection to God's existence. We do not claim to have a complete response to these difficult questions, but we hope to provide ways of thinking about them that at least lessen their power.

A second set of issues arises for believers around the question of how God acts in the world. If God creates the whole universe in a single act of creation, is there still room for God to "intervene" or act in particular events or occurrences in our life, such as miracles? In particular, can God respond to our prayers, or is such activity simply meaningless? In theological terms this is the question of providence, of God's ordering of creation in such a way as to allow for God's acting in the world. These are also questions we shall consider in this chapter.

A FINITE BUT PROVIDENT EMERGING WORLD ORDER

If we are going to discuss the problem of suffering and evil, we must begin by locating it within the world order that we have been discussing in previous chapters. We have seen from our previous discussions that our human existence is embedded in a world of emergent possibilities. The whole universe is evolving in accordance with both classical and statistical lawfulness, a universe of emerging schemes of recurrence, each with a finite probability of emergence and a finite probability of survival. Stars have fuel cycles that burn hydrogen and helium to produce heavier elements; planets orbit stars in seemingly endless cycles. Yet the fuel of the star can be exhausted, leading to a stellar collapse, followed by a supernova, which can then destroy the orbiting planets. Planets can become homes for the schemes of recurrence we call life, cycles of inception and predation, where new life forms emerge with a certain probability and can become extinct with a certain probability. And so a meteorite hitting the earth has apparently contributed to the extinction of the dinosaurs. Yet this very act of extinction allowed for the emergence of other life forms, the mammals, from which human beings have themselves emerged.

This is an incredibly complex web of interconnectedness and interdependence. Cosmologists have traced the possibilities for the origins of life to events in the first milliseconds of the universe. Some argue that the universe is "fine tuned" for life. If the universe had expanded more rapidly, stars and galaxies would not have formed, hence no planets and no life would exist. If it had expanded less rapidly, it would have collapsed in on itself before life could have occurred. Indeed, the balance between these two alternatives is very fine. Further, the chemicals of life, oxygen, carbon, iron, nitrogen, and so on, all had to be formed in stellar furnaces and expelled in violent supernova explosions.[3] Every nonhydrogen atom in our bodies was "cooked" inside a star that eventually went supernova.[4] Closer to home, astronomers note that, without the gas giants of Jupiter, Saturn, Uranus, and Neptune in our own solar system, our planet would have been continually bombarded by meteorites, making the emergence of life almost impossible. The gas giants act like huge gravitational vacuum cleaners, sweeping up meteors before they could do terminal damage to the life emerging on our planet.

And when we get to our own personal existence, it, too, has a fleetingly small probability of emergence. If our parents had not gone to that dance, if their parents had not met at the beach, and so on all the way back to the start of the human race—a small change in any of these precursor events and you or I simply would not exist. This is the depth of contingency we find in our world, in our very existence.[5] There is no you or I apart from the total world order that confronts us in creation. It is not as if God made all the component parts of creation and stuck them together to make the universe. Rather, the universe is an intelligible whole and our existence is inseparable from the existence of that whole. If we were to wind the clock back to the beginning of the Big Bang and then let the universe unfold once more, it is most unlikely that you or I would exist in this new universe. Or even that the Earth would exist!

As we saw in the previous chapter, there is an indeterminacy present in the unfolding of the universe even while there remains a directedness. The universe might well be fine tuned for life, as many cosmologists suggest, but that does not mean this form of life on this particular planet is preprogrammed to exist. Teleology is not deterministic in this way. Life has emerged according to a scheme of probabilities of emergence and of survival. Given the size and age of the universe, there is a strong statistical likelihood that somewhere life in various forms will emerge, but how and where and what type is an open question.[6]

Of course, this process of emergence is not all a pretty picture. Evolution incorporates the image of nature "red in tooth and claw."[7] Death, suffering, and extinction are all part of the whole. Death allows new life to emerge, extinction allows for new species. The same genetic variations that drive evolution can cause abnormalities and genetic diseases which lead to suffering and death. The same genetic variation that causes sickle-cell anemia provides some protection from malaria; the same genetic variation that leads to Type 1 diabetes provides some protection in times of famine. Many of nature's genetic "experiments" are simply aborted spontaneously before they can develop to birth. The same viruses and bacteria that "cull" the weak in the evolutionary struggle for the survival of the fittest can cause enormous pain and suffering to the living. And so on we can go. Our cosmos is not without its ambiguities.

PROVIDENCE AND THE GOODNESS OF CREATION

Still, with all these difficulties we can affirm the goodness of creation, of a world of emerging probability. The regularity of the schemes of recurrence that arise from the interaction of classical and statistical lawfulness provide stability and a degree of certainty about the future, without locking us into the regularity and monotony of a ticking clock. Probabilities of emergence allow for the creation of genuine novelty, of startling creativity and invention, new realities not reducible to their component parts. There is a directedness or finality to the process, the emergence of increasingly complex realities, schemes of schemes of schemes of recurrence, both stable and fragile, robust yet delicate.

For example, a human body can endure all types of hardship but be brought down by a simple virus. Indeed, human existence can be viewed as at the pinnacle of this process, because the schemes of recurrence that emerge here are not just biological but new patterns of meaning, truth, and value. Human beings create societies and cultures; they search for truth, scientifically, mathematically, philosophically, and theologically; they create works of art of enduring beauty; they love one another to the point of self-sacrifice. This process of human creation is itself a participation in the larger finality of the cosmos, an open-ended orientation become conscious, intelligent, and free, in the search for meaning, truth, goodness, and beauty. We explore the implications of this more fully in the next chapter.

In fact, one can argue that this human participation in the finality of the cosmos reveals the goal toward which that finality is headed. We are both its product and we participate in that finality, and our lives find their fulfillment not simply in biologically determined ends of eating, sleeping, and reproduction, but in an untiring orientation to meaning, truth, and goodness. Is such an orientation simply a huge cosmic joke played upon us by a meaningless and purposeless cosmos? Or does it point to One who is both the source of all meaning, truth, and goodness and who is the goal toward which we are ultimately oriented? As Aquinas would say, the One who is both source and goal, this One all people call God.

And so we affirm that God wills all this. God wills a universe of emergent probability, of evolution and all that it entails. God wills the whole and hence every part of the whole; God causes all this to exist as the primary cause of being, or, in more contemporary language, God is the source of all meaning, truth, and goodness. As our discussion indicates, however, God is not just the source but the goal or end toward which creation heads, with human existence being an exemplar, perhaps even the culmination, of that orientation. We find not only our source in God, but our fulfillment. Our existence, in all its finitude and suffering, is intrinsically related to the whole process. Without it we simply would not exist.

At the same time, like Job, we can protest against the whole thing. Has all this pain and suffering been worth it? The deeper question is: Could God create a world without them? Indeed, is it possible for God to create that which is not God, something that is finite and limited, yet not have pain and suffering? Given that any finite, limited, conscious being can suffer, it is difficult to know how suffering might not occur. Could God have created a world with less suffering? Probably so, but God could also create one with more suffering.[8] The question is whether suffering itself, not the amount, is sufficient to undermine the judgment of Genesis, that creation is "very good."

One important aspect of this emerging world is precisely the statistical nature of the events that drive emerging possibilities. Let us consider the problem of genetic disorders for a moment. Suppose the mechanism for genetic inheritance always worked perfectly, that it was no longer a statistical law governing reproduction but a classical "if-then" law. Then there would be no genetic variation through mutations, for example, and hence no genetic disorders such as sickle-cell anemia or cystic fibrosis. But then there would also be no development of new species, no evolution, or evidence of finality. Indeed, the world would look very different in every aspect, with perhaps no novelty at all possible in the cosmos. If God were to create such a world, it may well have been possible to create a world without suffering, but it would not look like the world we live in, nor would the act of creation itself be anything like what we know to be the case for our own cosmos. It might, in fact, be more like the world some creationists like to imagine, with God creating each species in its completeness without any evolutionary process.[9] While such a world without statistical lawfulness might be able to avoid aspects of the problem of suffering, it would also lack something else. In such a world there would be no possibility of freedom because we would live in a deterministic universe.

Providence is then the belief that the whole of world process is guided by divine intelligence, wisdom, and love, by God's loving wisdom and wise loving. God orders and wills the whole, and all the parts within the whole, through God's wisdom and love. In this sense, God does not "intervene" in creation *since God is never not acting.* The real difficulty is not to locate where God has responsibility for what we find in creation, but where God is not responsible. This is the really pressing issue in relation to the problem of evil, which we will consider shortly. God does not need to "tweak" creation, as some have proposed, to achieve particular outcomes.[10] Rather, God chooses the whole of creation, as the expression of divine wisdom and love, with those particular desired outcomes, from all possibilities available. Still, this does not reduce us to being mere puppets, with God pulling our strings. Secondary causes are real causes, including the secondary cause we call human freedom. But without the primary cause operating, giving us existence itself, all secondary causes would be nothing at all.

As the primary cause of being God suffuses the whole with meaning and goodness. Nonetheless, our grasp of the whole is limited and incomplete. We can grasp the goodness of a world of emergent possibilities, of regularity and novelty, and wonder at our own existence with its participation in the finality of the cosmos, orienting us to meaning, truth, and goodness, but it is this very orientation that allows us to question whether creation is really meaningful and good. When we experience the tragic elements of this creation, where the very processes that make life possible also lead to unexpected and painful destruction of life, we can call into question the meaning and purpose of the whole. But while we might protest at the suffering in the world, perhaps the final response we will get is that offered to Job in his complaints against God:

> Where were you when I laid the foundation of the earth?
>   Tell me, if you have understanding.
> Who determined its measurements—surely you know!
>   Or who stretched the line upon it?
> On what were its bases sunk,
>   or who laid its cornerstone
> when the morning stars sang together
>   and all the heavenly beings shouted for joy? (Job 38:4-7)

In the end we have no idea what it means to create a universe, or what might be possible or impossible in such a creation. While it is easy for us to imagine a world without suffering, such imaginings might not translate into a coherent and intelligible world order. If the whole is not intelligible, then such an imagined creation is a mere pipe dream, a fantasy, not realizable in fact.

This perhaps gives us some insight into what we mean by the notion of divine providence. While Jesus notes that every hair on our head has been counted, he also reminds us that God makes the sun shine and the rain fall on the good and bad alike. Providence does not protect good people from suffering, nor does it inflict suffering on the wicked. Suffering is an inescapable part of life that we all must face, to varying degrees, with integrity, courage, and compassion. Suffering may be an occasion for weakness and sin, or of heroic courage and determination. Some rise above their sufferings to become sources of inspiration, hope, and love for others. Others, sadly, sink into despair and depression. And we are all called to respond with compassion for those caught in suffering, to assist them to relieve their suffering and know that they remain valued members of the human community whatever their situation might be. To believe in divine providence is to face all such situations with trust in God, that God's love will be sufficient for us to manage and that we perhaps might even grow from our experience.

PROVIDENCE AND PRAYER

Before we go on to explore the question of human freedom and its relationship to the problem of suffering and evil, there remains one question that requires attention. If God's relationship to the world is as we have described it, is there a point to prayer? Can our prayer change God's mind and produce a different outcome than if we had not prayed? Of course, we would not want to suggest that God can be manipulated in some sense—that if we pray in the right way we can guarantee a desired outcome, like winning the lottery. But Jesus does encourage us to pray and assures us that God listens to and responds to our prayers.

Much of the problem, of course, lies in our continued imaginative attempt to place God within a temporal frame. If I pray "now" I can change God's mind "now" and achieve some desired outcome "then." However, God is not in time. And so the question is, Can an eternal, unchanging God respond to prayer? Indeed, one could argue that God responds eternally to our prayer. In the one divine act of creation, which encompasses past, present, and future (for us), God has chosen a creation in wisdom and love that responds to our prayers in precisely the way God has willed. We may witness this through a course of events (possibly happy coincidences) or simply through a change in our own attitudes to these events. It may be that our prayers bring God into a situation in a way that God would otherwise not be there. But this itself is something God knows eternally in the act of creation. And if we had not so prayed God would not have so responded. So prayer remains meaningful.

We, being in space and time, cannot fathom the reasons behind God's answers to our prayers. But every prayer has implicit within it, "Thy will be done." Thus, rather than praying to "change God's mind," in prayer we put ourselves in God's hands and trust God's loving will for the whole. We invite God into our realities whatever they are, whether, for example, a loved one is "spared" or "taken" in a car accident. Furthermore, this very invitation on our part can serve to bring about change to the situation. Our prayers themselves thus contribute to God's providence in the here and now.

Indeed, an eternal unchanging God is not thereby a remote God. If we pose the question in terms of "How is a transcendent God close to us?" we seem to inevitably attempt to place God somehow within space and time, in much the manner of process thought. However, if we turn the question around and ask, "How are we close to God?," then we are eternally and intimately close to God who knows and loves us into being. For God our existence is an integral element of the whole of creation, willed eternally in the one divine act of creation. As the psalmist states:

> O Lord, you have searched me and known me.
> You know when I sit down and when I rise up;
>   you discern my thoughts from far away.
> You search out my path and my lying down,
>   and are acquainted with all my ways.
> Even before a word is on my tongue,
>   O Lord, you know it completely.
> You hem me in, behind and before,
>   and lay your hand upon me.
> Such knowledge is too wonderful for me;
>   it is so high that I cannot attain it. (Ps. 139:1-6)

PAIN, SUFFERING, AND EVIL

We can now turn our attention to the question of suffering and evil in the world. Years ago when the popular psychological author M. Scott Peck was planning to write a book on the problem of evil, he reported that people would say to him things like, "Maybe you will help me to understand my son's cerebral palsy." He would respond by distinguishing between what we might call "natural evil" and "moral evil." His work was concerned with the latter.[11] The point he was seeking to make is that there is a major difference between the problem of suffering and the problem of evil. It is very important to learn to distinguish these because in our own culture we have come to conflate the two, often thinking of suffering itself as the only form of evil.

So let us begin with some distinctions. First, we can talk about pain. We all experience pain to some degree or another, from minor aches to more serious trauma. We share pain with other animals and it is an important biological mechanism warning us of potential or actual damage to our bodies. The presence of pain alerts us to the need to act, to take our hand off the hot plate, to avoid the sharp object, lest greater damage be done. As such, pain has a meaning and purpose biologically, no matter how uncomfortable we may be about it. Certainly, most of us put up with the minor aches and pains of life as a nuisance but not as something that detracts from the purpose and goodness of existence. However, we can also talk about suffering as a particularly human experience of pain. Such suffering emerges as we struggle to make sense of experiences of pain and limitation. Pain can overwhelm us and impinge on our life plans or even our day-to-day functioning. It can rob us of pleasure and joy in life. In such situations we can ask, "Why me?" What meaning or purpose could this suffering have? Here the experience of pain becomes an experience of a lack of meaning that we feel acutely. This same sense of lack of meaning can accompany difficult emotional situations that may not involve physical pain but do produce suffering, such as relationship breakdowns. And so the notion of suffering goes beyond pain itself to become a human category, as pain and limitation are taken up into a world of meaning and value. And, of course, many people have dealt with their suffering by seeking meaning that helps them find real purpose for their lives. There are also occasions where we may endure pain willingly, as when a physiotherapist stretches our muscles and joints, in order to alleviate greater pain later on.

Finally, we can talk about moral evil. Moral evil is very different. It arises in the decision to turn from the truly good and to embrace an apparent or lesser good. Sometimes this may be a cause of pain and suffering for others, at other times it might not. Still, when we encounter evil it can raise for us the same questions that are raised in the cases of pain and suffering—"Why is this happening?"—because, in the end, evil, too, is a problem of a deficit in meaning. But its "cause" is quite different. We can approach this through Augustine's attempt to grasp the nature of evil.

The problem of evil was a great concern to Augustine in the fourth and fifth centuries. He asked, *Unde malum?*—"Whence evil?" He framed the problem as follows: if evil has a cause, then either God is the cause (as the cause of all existence) which is abhorrent, or God is not the cause of everything, and the alternate cause of evil is a force equal to and opposed to God (dualism). For a part of his life Augustine followed such a dualist belief called Manichaeism. He eventually overcame this dilemma, however, by arguing that evil has no cause, an argument he develops in Book 7 of the *Confessions*. In fact, this is precisely why it is evil. Why do we choose evil over good? There is no reasonableness to the choice. Reason itself directs us to the good, so when we choose evil it is because we have not followed the dictates of reason. What Augustine is stating when he says evil has "no substance" is that evil has no reason. It lacks that which is constitutive of reality, that is, sufficient reason. Evil is thus a privation of the good, the good of sufficient reason to be.

Augustine has already prepared us for this metaphysical conclusion in Book 2 of the *Confessions*, in the story of the pear tree, where he and a group of friends steal some pears only to then throw them against a wall. There Augustine scrutinizes this childhood misdemeanor with a penetrating interrogation as to his motives for his action. He begins his account with a blunt acknowledgment that his action had "*no reason . . .* there was *no motive* for my malice except malice."[12] Indeed, the whole analysis of his and others' actions revolves around the notion of motivation, or reasons for one's actions. "People look for *the reason* why some criminal act has been committed."[13] In his critical self-examination he finds "nothing": "I found nothing to love save the theft itself."[14] In the end he finds his own actions unintelligible: "Who understands his faults?"[15] This lack of reasonable motivation or intelligibility for the act is the psychological correlate of Augustine's metaphysical analysis of evil as lacking substance or reality.

Of course, this is not to say evil does not "exist," as if we have simply denied the reality of the problem altogether. Rather, we are talking about its mode of existence as a privation or lack of something. As Herbert McCabe puts it in his book *God Matters*, "Now does this mean that badness is unreal? Certainly not. Things really are bad sometimes and this is because the absence of what is expected is just as real as a presence. If I have a hole in my sock, the hole is not anything at all, it is just an absence of wool or cotton or whatever, but it is a perfectly real hole in my sock."[16] And, of course, it is just as annoying!

In more modern terms we might try to think of evil in terms of its meaninglessness or pointlessness. When confronted with great moral evil, such as the destruction of the World Trade Center on 9/11, it strikes us as so disproportionate, so counterproductive, so pointless in its taking of innocent lives, that we find it incomprehensible. And this is the point about evil. It is incomprehensible precisely because it is deficient or lacking in meaning. We simply cannot get our heads around what happened. It defies all our attempts to understand. And so we can talk about a genuine mystery of evil, a mystery that lacks any intelligibility.[17] In a very real sense not even God knows why we sin.

And so we can see both the distinction and the overlap between the problems of suffering and evil. Suffering is a human experience of a lack of meaning in our encounter with pain and finitude. On the one hand, sometimes we suffer because we cannot grasp what meaning our experience might have; it eludes us, not because it has no meaning, but because that meaning may be hidden from us. This, too, is part of our condition of finitude, and in such situations all we may be able to do is trust in a provident God to make sense of our situation where we cannot. On the other hand, we may suffer because there really is no meaning here to grasp. We are confronted with genuine moral evil, a radical lack of meaning for which even God can find no meaning. Of course, when we are in such situations it can be difficult to know which is which.

Nonetheless, it is important to maintain the distinction. If we do not, we move in one of two directions. We may identify moral evil with finitude; we think that because we cannot find meaning there is no meaning to be found. Those holding this view assume that somehow creation itself is the problem. There have been various manifestations of this throughout the centuries, but the common name for them is "dualism." Dualism holds that materiality itself is evil—spirit is good, bodies are bad; hence, sexuality is bad. Death actually frees the spirit from the limitations of embodiment. Often dualists will distance God from responsibility for the material order, finding its origin in something other than God, for example, a lesser deity or even the devil. Dualism is precisely what the biblical authors rejected when they stated, "God saw everything that he had made, and indeed, it was very good" (Gen. 1:31).

Dualism is precisely what the early church rejected when it insisted on the full incarnation of Jesus. Still, it can be difficult to maintain a belief in the goodness of creation in the face of severe pain and suffering.

Alternatively, we may consider evil and good to be merely two complementary sides of a coin. The radical disjunction between good and evil, and the lack of intelligibility that is at the heart of evil, is not acknowledged. The resolution of the problem of evil becomes, then, merely that of accepting both as part of created existence. One seeks to find a "balance between good and evil" (Carl Jung) or a position "beyond good and evil" (Friedrich Nietzsche). Or we assume that evil is simply a product of our finitude, perhaps a matter of social conditioning, or our genetic make-up, or something else that excuses our action. In this approach no one is held to account, no one is responsible for their actions, and everyone is always trying their best under the circumstances at hand.

FREE WILL IN AN EMERGENT WORLD

Let us now return to the question of human freedom. We have already noted how human existence is itself the product of the finality evident in the cosmos. Further, our human participation in this finality reveals it to be oriented to meaning, truth, and goodness. This orientation, which is manifest in human knowing and willing, is itself a form of statistical lawfulness. It is not governed by a deterministic rule, always giving the same outcome with the same inputs. Nor is it simply "random" or arbitrary. As one element in that orientation, human willing or freedom has its own inherent orientation to the good, an orientation that is successful in achieving the good according to a certain statistical probability. The more virtuous the person, the more successful the orientation will be; the more vicious, the less successful. Indeed, virtues and vices are themselves schemes of recurrence, or what we might call "habits," incorporating biological, psychological, and volitional elements. As schemes of recurrence they emerge with a certain probability and survive with a certain probability. Virtues increase the probability of a person acting morally while vices increase the probability of acting immorally. Virtues are particular ways in which we embody aspects of human flourishing.[18]

The idea that human freedom has a fundamental orientation to the good runs counter to our cultural conception of freedom as arbitrary choice.

Freedom as "freedom of choice" emphasizes the fact that we do in fact have alternative courses of action open to us. There is no strictly deterministic law operating in our choices. However, freedom is not then just "arbitrary" choice. It, too, is governed by a statistical form of lawfulness, which we can think of as an orientation. As an orientation, it does not compel us or create a necessity but it does shift the probabilities in one direction or another. This orientation to the good grounds the possibility of distinguishing between good and bad choices. If choice were strictly arbitrary then how would we make such a distinction? Attending to that orientation, what might be called "conscience," allows us to distinguish good from bad.[19]

In fact, given that freedom of choice is so highly valued, it often seems that the mere fact of our choosing something is sufficient justification for the goodness of the choice. On the position here developed, however, freedom is not self-justifying; rather, choices are justified by adopting an orientation to the good. Good decisions are justified by good reasons, by a commitment to the good; bad decisions cannot make such an appeal to good reasons, but to excuses and rationalizations, whose lack of honesty is readily exposed by the simple task of asking the right questions.

Of course, freedom is a great good. Freedom lies at the heart of human dignity. Our freedom can be viewed as a participation in the divine freedom. We become co-creators with God; our "dominion" over the world is expressed in our freedom to create not only a wide variety of technologies to manipulate the world but also a large variety of human societies, cultures, art forms, philosophies, and so on. What intelligence can conceive, we can set about achieving, from better computers to more just societies. Most importantly, we shape our own personal existence. Our acts of freedom shape our future acts; we are both a self who determines through our freedom, and a self who is determined or shaped by the exercise of our freedom. Virtue builds on virtue, strengthening our orientation to the good, while vice "builds" on vice, blinding us further to the good. We shall consider further the implications of this for understanding morality in the next chapter.

And so the perversion of the greater good is the greater evil. Freedom is a great good, but its perversion is sin and the moral evil that flows from sin. Again, we are faced with a similar question that arose with the problem of suffering. Given the amount of evil in the world—pornography, sex assault and abuse, inequitable trade conditions, indebtedness beyond measure in third-world countries, the arms trade, environmental destruction, and so on— is it all worth it? Does not the injustice of it all cry out to heaven? Is the great good of freedom worth all the evil that such freedom allows to occur?

EVIL AND RESPONSIBILITY

While the questions are similar, the response will be quite different with regard to moral evil. In dealing with the question of pain and suffering we found that there was a reasonableness about suffering. Pain and the suffering it causes occur because of our finitude. They have a purpose or meaningfulness in terms of seeking to alert us to dangers and protecting us from greater harm. In that sense the possibility and actuality of suffering are part of the universe that God creates. Sin and moral evil, however, do not have such a purpose or meaningfulness. In fact, it is evil precisely because of this lack. This is not to say it completely lacks any intended meaningfulness, but it arises from a lack of purpose sufficient to justify the act. This scenario is what Augustine meant when he argued that evil has no substance. It is a lack of meaning or purpose that should be there but is not. The evil is the "no-thing," the disparity between the purpose and meaning of the person acting and what would be needed to justify the act undertaken.[20] Such a disparity has no cause; what should cause us to act is sufficient reason to do so. The evil act has no cause sufficient for the act, and so has no cause. It is our failure in the realm of achieving the good.

We might consider the situation, sadly too common in our world, of terrorist acts. After such atrocities we often hear of terrorist groups "claiming responsibility." Yet the act itself was irresponsible, an unjust targeting of innocent people. In a basic sense it lacked a fundamental orientation to meaning, truth, and goodness. It failed to ask relevant questions or maintain the basic value of life, especially of the innocent. How does one claim responsibility for an irresponsible act? Yes, they initiated the act, but they were not responsible *in* the act, though they may be responsible *for* the act. This is the paradox of human freedom. We are responsible for our own lack of responsibility.

This leads to important conclusions in terms of divine responsibility. As we have argued, God is the cause of all that exists. But moral evil is the gap between what is and what ought to be. This gap results from a failure to seek the good. This failure in us is a failure to be moved by good reasons.

In that sense we are acting as a deficient cause. God is not the cause of this deficiency simply because it has no cause. Whatever exists is caused to be by God, but evil is the lack or hole in being, the "being" of good reasons. So while God can be thought of as an indirect cause of pain and the suffering that results, as a primary cause of all that is, God cannot be thought of as the cause of evil.

And so we can ask, Why is there evil anyway? Perhaps the most shocking response is that, in fact, it has no answer. Why evil occurs is a fundamental enigma, and one that completely lacks an intelligent answer. Even God cannot answer the question as to why someone sins. No satisfactory response can be found that would provide an insight into the question. The enigma of sin remains obscure even to God. One might perhaps weaken the question by asking, rather, "Why does God allow evil?" After all, God chooses this creation, which happens to contain evil. One response to this objection is to state that God does not endorse evil; in fact, God forbids it through the moral law: "hate what is evil, hold fast to what is good" (Rom. 12:9), the Ten Commandments, the natural law, and so on. So God enjoins us to resist sin and to turn toward the good. God does not "allow evil."

Finally, we might weaken the question even further, "Why does God create a world in which moral evil might occur?" Now, human freedom is a great good; with freedom certainly comes the possibility of sin. However, there is a gap between the possibility and the actuality of sinning. Is it possible for God to have made a universe in which, in fact, no one ever sinned? Perhaps, but even so, in a world where sin occurs, responsibility for that sin remains with the sinner, not God. Certainly, God could have made a world without freedom, but freedom is among the highest created values, a great good. And freedom includes the possibility of sin. Further, the fact of evil, unintelligible though it is, makes possible a new type of good, that of mercy, forgiveness, and redemption. This is not a "reason" for evil, or even for allowing evil, but a response to evil. In the end all we can really assert is that, despite the presence and fact of evil, this creation is still good; indeed, it is very good. Again, as Lonergan writes, we are called to an act of trust in God: "Without faith, without the eye of love, the world is too evil for God to be good, for a good God to exist. But faith recognizes that God grants men their freedom, that he wills them to be persons and not just his automata, that he calls them to the higher authenticity that overcomes evil with good."[21] And it is to the problem of responding to evil that we must now turn.

THE DIVINELY ORIGINATED SOLUTION TO THE PROBLEM OF EVIL

We have considered above the notion that evil is the lack or gap in being that arises from a failure to act with sufficient reason or cause. The alternate view of evil is that it is somehow real or "substantial." When this is the case the solution to the problem of evil is either to destroy the evil "thing" or to segregate oneself from it. On the one hand, if only we could destroy evil or cut ourselves off from it, then only the pure and good would remain. Sinners in particular should be excluded because they have been contaminated by evil. On the other hand, if evil is a lack, something that is missing that should be there, then the solution to the problem of evil is to make up for what is lacking, to repair the damage done, and turn the evil act into an opportunity for a greater good, the good of conversion, forgiveness, and mercy. And so we can now consider the question, If God is indeed good, what if anything is God doing about the problem of evil?[22]

We have considered the ways in which the natural world is the product of both classical and statistical lawfulness, an emergent world of novelty but also of failings. There are probabilities of emergence and of survival. Human beings have emerged into an emerging world to become part of this larger process of emergence. Through human intelligence and creativity we have learned to construct our own schemes of recurrence, our technological, economic, political, and cultural orders, the very stuff of human history. This has led us from being primitive hunter-gatherers operating in tribal groupings, to being able to manipulate our own genetic code, to being able to transmit sound and image instantaneously around the globe from our desks, to creating powerful nation-states and truly global economic, political, and cultural institutions.

However, while there has been remarkable progress in so many areas, there have also been destructive and incomprehensible elements of decline. From the dawn of human history there has been conflict driven by a desire to dominate, a *libido dominandi*, resulting in incalculable violence and destruction. In the last century this resulted in two world wars, with millions of lives lost and a legacy of nuclear weapons that are an ongoing threat to human survival. Meanwhile, our very economic success is resulting in a litany of environmental concerns, of water and air quality, of greenhouse gases, soil erosion, toxic by-products from industry, and so on. While initially some of these problems arise out of our ignorance of the impact we are having, once the impact is known and documented, to fail to act to remove or mitigate these effects begins to move into the realm of the unintelligibility of evil. This is the problem of evil writ large into human history, a problem that now can threaten the very viability of life on our planet.

Is God in fact doing something about this history of decline, of evil and its impact on humanity? What might such a solution look like, a divinely originated solution to the problem of evil? Certainly, it would be accessible to all peoples in some sense, yet also operate according to the same principles of emergence, with a certain probability of emerging and of surviving in the struggles with forces of evil in human history. It would assist human beings by strengthening their basic orientation to the good (*charity*), giving them a *hope* that can overcome the dangers of despair in the face of widespread decline, and help them better understand their place in God's creation and the divine will for their redemption (*faith*). And it would take instances of human evil and seek to transform them into opportunities for a greater good, the good of conversion, forgiveness, and mercy.

This process of transformation is rarely undertaken without cost, for it requires the one who is the victim of evil to transcend the impulse to return evil with evil, violence with violence, and instead to turn the other cheek, to love one's enemies, to offer forgiveness to those who persecute them. This inevitably involves a willingness to suffer for the sake of the other. Here we find a different possible relationship between pain and suffering on the one hand, and evil on the other. Far from pain and suffering being a punishment for evil, or being identified with evil, they can, paradoxically, become a means for overcoming evil. Christians find this best expressed in the life and death of Jesus. Jesus' willingness to suffer and die for us is an embodied expression of his teaching in the Sermon on the Mount, to turn the other cheek, to love one's enemies, and to offer forgiveness to those who persecute us. Suffering of this sort can unmask and disempower evil, revealing it in is banality and meaninglessness.[23]

Of course, this is not to promote "suffering in silence" or passivity in the face of evil. This is powerfully brought out in *Gandhi*, director Richard Attenborough's 1982 film version of the life of Mahatma Gandhi (also an important reminder that this insight into evil and suffering is not restricted to Christians).[24] In the film one of Gandhi's colleagues accuses him of promoting "passive resistance," to which he replies, "I, for one, have never advocated passive anything." His doctrine of active resistance is illustrated in a powerful scene centered around a salt mine. Salt production was controlled and taxed by the British, but was an essential part of life in India given the hot climate. A group of protesters line up outside a salt mine to attempt entry as a protest against the British policy. As they march forward, they are beaten by guards, then carried off and cared for by supporters. They continue to march forward despite the beatings. To the side an American reporter files his story on a phone: "They walked, with heads up, without music, or cheering, or any hope of escape from injury or death. It went on and on and on. Women carried the wounded bodies from the ditch until they dropped from exhaustion. But still it went on. Whatever moral ascendance the West held was lost today. India is free for she has taken all that steel and cruelty can give, and she has neither cringed nor retreated."

The protesters' willingness to suffer exposes the moral bankruptcy of the British Empire. Gandhi's strategy of active resistance seeks to expose the pointlessness of their continued occupancy of the continent and set India on the path to independence. Yet it is done in a spirit of conciliation and forgiveness: "We have come a long way together with the British. When they leave we want to see them off as friends."

Nonetheless, while acknowledging that others may share this insight, for Christians the divinely originated solution to the problem of evil is found with greatest clarity in the life and death of Jesus and in the community of disciples who follow in his footsteps. It is most evident in the lives of those holy men and women who have done as Jesus did, offering their lives for the sake of others. As the life of both Jesus and Gandhi demonstrate, this loving sacrifice of resistance has the power to change history, to shift us from decline and restore the path of genuine progress. In the end the problem of evil is a practical problem requiring a practical solution. This practical solution lies at the heart of the Gospel.

CONCLUSION

Throughout this work we have sought to maintain that the understanding of God found in the classical theological tradition remains a robust account of the relationship between God and creation. Certainly, it is adequate to the questions posed by contemporary science. In this chapter we have addressed the more difficult problems of pain, suffering, and evil, within a view of the whole of creation as the work of a provident God. As we saw at the beginning of the chapter, proclaiming certain individual events to be the work of God's intervening providence runs the risk of making God a secondary cause, raises difficult further questions, and is ultimately inadequate at a pastoral level. It is unlikely that our account would convince those without faith, but we hope that for those with religious faith it might provide some insight, without offense to those without faith. Central to our account has been a world of emerging possibilities that does not fit into a strict "if-then" approach, a world where statistical lawfulness is built into world process. This also raises questions about the ways in which we make decisions, about human morality. These we take up in the next chapter.

CHAPTER 6

IMPLICATIONS FOR HUMAN LIVING: MORAL AGENCY AND EMERGENT PROBABILITY

NOVA is an American television show on matters scientific. In 2009 it produced a three-part series entitled "Becoming Human: Unearthing Our Earliest Ancestors," which traces human lineage through its many and varied species over millions of years. One exciting moment stands out: Meave and Richard Leakey, in 1984, uncovering an almost complete skeleton of a young boy who died 1.6 million years ago. Found near Lake Turkana in Kenya, he was quickly dubbed "Turkana boy." The documentary shows Meave Leakey, years later at this famed site, recalling how excited she was to realize the profundity of what they had found.[1]

This image, of a matron of paleontology waxing eloquent about the skeleton of a young boy who had lived almost two million years previously and its role in aid of understanding of our ancestry, serves as an icon of what it means to be human. Only humans can ponder our own heritage. Only humans have expended entire life careers digging in the dirt to uncover clues to what came before us.

A second and equally profound moment came in 2010, when a collaboration of scientists from around the world was able to extract a small segment of DNA from a bone specimen from a Neanderthal skeleton. While these bones are not as old as those of Turkana boy—a mere thirty thousand years—this magnificent accomplishment, only recently possible, involved sequencing the genome of this ancient relative.[2] The ability to sequence nucleotides in human DNA has only been available in the last decade. That scientists could apply this technology to human remains that are over thirty thousand years old is truly a remarkable advance in human understanding.

These examples of humans seeking to grasp the complexities of their own history illustrate what makes our species—*Homo sapiens*—so distinctive. As Erich Fromm once put it: "Man is the only animal for whom his own existence is a problem he has to solve."[3] Indeed, the very writing and reading of this book illustrates exactly this fact: humans have evolved to the point at which they are self-reflexive enough to ponder their own existence and raise questions about what kind of Creator, if any, might be the source of it all.

In the previous chapter we introduced the conundrum of human freedom and, at times, its malicious effects. In this chapter we will continue to explore the human as agent—as actor and contributor to her own future. Initially, we will examine the nature of human emergence and how emergent probability operates as an aspect of culture. We will then go on to show how the intersection of chance and order works out in human living—delineating an "ethic of risk" in relation to an "ethic of control." We will provide examples of how certain human actions can and have established new conditions of possibility for transformation. Finally, we will elaborate how this ethic of risk can be understood as a co-operation with God's providential will and the implications this has for resolving the problem of evil.

HOMO SAPIENS: WHAT MAKES US SO SPECIAL?

As we have mentioned earlier, what is striking about human genetics is the degree to which our DNA is similar to that of other species. The nucleotide pairs in the human genome sequence are in the same order as those in chimps 98.8 percent of the time. The genetic similarity between humans and mice is 96 percent. So what makes us so different?[4]

It seems that our physical evolution has occurred in the same way that it has in other mammals. Specifically, we are descended from apes, our most recent common ancestor being chimpanzees. Over many, many thousands of years, incremental changes in our tool kit of genes, combined with external environmental forces, have culled our ancestry in the direction of adaptive traits. Specifically human features include upright posture, large brains (relative to body size), symbolic language and speech, opposable thumbs, as well as the development of tool use and cultural expression.

Approximately six million years ago (from here on abbreviated as MYA) the hominin line (human ancestry) split off from the hominid (humans and apes) trajectory. Even so, it took another four million years for the genus *Homo* to emerge. Turkana boy seems to have been at the cusp of this shift two MYA—not fully ape yet not quite human. *Homo sapiens*, our own species within this genus, has been around for a mere 200,000 years. Currently, scholars believe there have been between fifteen to twenty different hominin species that have emerged in the six million years since the human line diverged from ape ancestors. Our own *Homo sapiens* species is the only one still existent, once the Neanderthal line died out thirty thousand years ago.[5]

There are two things to note about these timeframes. First, there is the extremely long time it took for our own human line to develop.[6] If we think back to the birth of Christ two thousand years ago, we would have to multiply that time by three thousand to get to the dawn of the hominin lines. We would have to multiply by one hundred just to get to the beginning of the *Homo sapiens* line. Second, we need to note that the history of *Homo sapiens* is a mere fraction of the history of hominins. Our species has been around only 3 percent of the total time span of hominin evolution. While we may be special, our emergence, like that of other species, has taken place over many, many generations, with multiple other human species emerging and disappearing in the process.

As for distinctively human characteristics, bipedalism goes back a long way. In 1976 another astonishing find in Tanzania revealed two sets of footprints preserved in hardened volcanic ash. Nearly 3.6 MYA an adult and a child walked together, upright, through this ash. More or less the same age as the infamous Lucy—an *Australopithecus afarensis* specimen found in Ethiopia—these show that walking upright emerged early on in hominin evolution.

The development of large brains is another matter. Both brain and body size increased dramatically in the genus *Homo* since the era of Turkana boy approximately two MYA. The increase in both appears to have come in fits and starts, with a period of relative stasis for about one million years in the middle. What counts, in evolutionary terms, is not brain or body size per se but relative brain size given body size. While it is not clear exactly what advantages larger brains gave to the genus *Homo*, several periods of climate change seem to have presented challenges to survival. Those species more able to adapt to the constantly changing conditions of food availability, water needs, hunting, and migration are the ones who survived and passed their adaptive advantages on to further generations.[7]

TABLE 6.1 BRAIN AND BODY SIZE EVOLUTION IN HOMININS[8]

Species	Estimated Age (MYA)[9]	Body Size (Kg)	Brain size (Cm3)	Ratio of brain size to body size
Homo sapiens	0-0.2	53	1355	25.57
H. neanderthalensis	0.03-0.3	76	1512[10]	19.90
H. heidelbergensis	~0.3-0.4	62	1198	19.32
H. erectus	0.2-1.9	57	1016	17.82
H. ergaster (Turkana Boy)	1.5-1.9	58	854	14.72
H. habilis	1.6-2.3	34	552	16.24
Paranthropus boisei	1.2-2.2	44	510	11.60
Australopithecus africanus	2.6-3.0	36	457	12.70
Au. aferensis (Lucy)	3.0-3.6	NA	NA	
Au. Animensis	3.5-4.1	NA	NA	
Ardipithecis ramidus kadabba	5.2-5.8	NA	NA	
Sahellanthropus tchadensis	6-7	NA	~320-380	

Not least in the advantages that came with larger brains was the development of tool use, interwoven with cultural developments. Deep in the bowels of the Spanish mountains there is a "pit of bones" that has revealed skeletal remains dating back 500,000 years. This discovery is notable, not only because it yielded thirty complete skeletons of Neanderthal ancestors, but because it appears that these corpses were intentionally buried—even with some ceremony. Among the bones was found a hand ax made of pink quartz—a material that would have come from far away. It seems that both tools and symbolic actions, such as ceremonial burials, go a long way back in hominin history.[11]

Indeed, tool use is documented as far back as *Homo habilis*, 2.5 MYA. Decorative art, using red ochre pigment, along with seashells with holes drilled in them, have been found in caves in South Africa, from approximately 75,000 years ago. The same group that lived here made a technological leap when they began heating materials to make tools 71,000 years ago. Further, it seems that the demise of the Neanderthal race 30,000 years ago, and the survival, in contrast, of *Homo sapiens*, is tied to both climate change and technology. Neanderthals, over their 270,000-year history, had become experts in the killing of large mammals. They killed them with hand-held spears. With climate change and the dying off of these large mammals, Neanderthals were unable to adapt, while *Homo sapiens*, who had devised projectile spears that could be thrown to kill smaller, faster game at a distance, survived.

Thus human evolution follows the trajectory of evolution in other animals—over long, long periods of time, chance mutations in concert with climatic and environmental pressures shifted probabilities in favor of adaptive traits.[12] In the case of humans, these traits included upright posture and larger brains such that tool making, symbolic cultures, and intentional planning became regularities. So we arrive at modern *Homo sapiens* who can question their own existence and execute scholarly projects to understand their own ancestry. As Emerson Pugh, an IBM researcher, once said: "If the human brain were so simple that we could understand it, we would be so simple that we couldn't."[13] The human brain is not simple and we have now established intricate cultures, technologies, and patterns of cooperation that are both the result of and the drivers of evolution.

In earlier chapters we elucidated the notion of emergent probability as the interaction of order and chance over time. Schemes of recurrence provide predictable and recurrent cycles of physical, chemical, biological, and neurological processes. Yet these themselves are the product of chance interacting with order, and continue to be conditionally dependent on the manifold of relations that undergird them. If *Homo sapiens* have moved evolution beyond happenstance to intentional acts of inquiry and technology, how do human actions, the stuff of history and culture, fit into this explanation of emergent probability?

What is true of atoms, bacteria, insects, plants, and animals is all the more true of human life, relationships, and behavior. There are regularities—schemes of recurrence—that function according to a series of directly causal events; from individual habits of personal hygiene to the laws and practices governing traffic patterns. Generally, we notice these patterns of recurrent behavior only if they break down, as when we have a toothache or get stranded overnight in an airport. While there are many orderly patterns of human conduct and meaning that perpetuate themselves, these patterns are not inevitable but depend on the persistence of underlying conditions.

Furthermore, human affairs fall under emergent probability in a distinctive way. Though human schemes emerge and reach a stability whereby they function routinely, as human life develops, less and less importance becomes attached to mere circumstance and more and more importance is attached to the operation of human intelligence and choice. The significant probabilities become not those of emerging physical, chemical, biological, or zoological systems, but those of the occurrence of insight, communication, persuasion, consensus, cooperation, and action. Rather than being merely "conditioned by" our environments, humans are "conditioners of" our environments and, hence, of ourselves. While this is true of many, if not all, living species, it is true in an unprecedented way of *Homo sapiens*, agents who grasp meaning and transform our worlds through action.[14]

So "survival of the fittest" as it operates at the biological level takes a different turn with more recent human species. Human life is not merely a matter of biological survival and reproduction but has to do with the meaning and values that we ascribe to our living. The schemes of recurrence that make our lives possible have to do with habits of meaning, regular choices of value, an antecedent willingness to opt for value when value and satisfaction conflict. Survival is not only about physical existence and reproduction. It is also about the survival of meaning, of purpose in life, of self-esteem and dignity, of communities of cooperative interaction.

Examples of patterns of cooperation and meaning—the schemes of recurrence that drive human life—abound. The work of the Leakeys and the genomic research that has unveiled our relation to the Neanderthals are all built on an elaborate infrastructure that makes education, research, travel, and scholarship possible. The very way humans eat is saturated with meaning—we set a table, light candles, garnish platters of food to make them look nice, and have manners by which we partake of our dinners. Food even plays a role in religious meaning. Judaism prescribes some foods as kosher and has many rituals that take place around the family table. Ramadan, a month of fasting in Islam, ends with the celebration of Eid. And eating bread and wine—the Eucharist—has been central to Christian worship since its earliest days.

The survival of meaning is dependent, of course, on the material resources that make physical survival possible, but the presence of such material resources is itself dependent on systems of schemes of recurrence that have been created by human industry, intention, and meaning. Thus promoting life has to do with promoting the conditions for the possibility of dignity, value, community, loving intersubjectivity. To the degree that egoism, group bias, prejudice, or a quest for mere power distort these underlying conditions to favor some to the exclusion of others, survival of the fittest means that some, literally, survive at the expense of others. Perhaps more profoundly, some claim personhood, meaning, and self-value at the expense of others' dignity.[15] So we come to the arena of ethics, of the human agency that chooses, and in so choosing creates conditions of possibility for the flourishing or demise of both human and nonhuman existence.

THE QUESTION OF SOUL AND SPIRIT IN EVOLUTIONARY TERMS

To discuss the evolution of human beings raises questions about when human beings developed a "soul" or became "spiritual." Or, more directly, when did human beings become "human" in the theological sense of being created in the image and likeness of God?

The perspective developed in this work, of emergent probability, acknowledges the possibility of the emergence of something distinctively new, something that is not reducible to its underlying components. What we witness in the history of human evolution is the emergence of a defining orientation toward meaning, truth, and goodness. This is a new occurrence, something not evident in nonhuman species. When it precisely occurred we cannot be certain, but the evidence of its presence is found in the brief outline above—the use of tools, the beginning of language, of art, and, notably, of a concern with death and burial. At some stage in human evolution, this orientation to meaning, truth, and goodness became the central defining characteristic of human existence, and not just a random occurrence.

This orientation, which is a conscious and intelligent participation in the overarching finality of the universe, is what is meant by the traditional theological language of soul or spirit. While its emergence bears some relationship to underlying material conditions, as noted above concerning brain size relative to body weight, there is also a certain independence from these underlying conditions. Brain size is not a direct measure of intelligence. At the same time, this central spiritual orientation remains dependent on the integrity of the underlying components. And so alcohol not only affects our brain chemistry but lowers our intelligence and makes our decisions less reliable. Likewise, given our orientation to meaning, truth, and goodness, we must learn to integrate all our lower-order systems into a meaningful whole, a way of life. In this way we are conditioners of our own futures in a unique way. This distinctive moral agency and how it unfolds thus warrants further consideration.

MORAL AGENCY, DECISION MAKING, CONTROL, AND RISK

Throughout this book we have been delineating a new worldview, one that is grounded, we believe, in the concrete reality of the way the world unfolds. It is a worldview that is the fruit of several centuries of transition from a deterministic world driven by stable and unchanging laws to a perspective in which dynamism, change, and chance are operative. Now, just as our understanding of the nonhuman world has had to move away from assumptions of determinism, so, too, does our conception of human agency. Human actions are not merely about directly causal chains of events. Rather, just as other aspects of the world are subject to probabilities, so our choosing involves us in discerning possible outcomes of our actions and shifting probabilities for change. We begin with a discussion of an "ethic of control" in contrast to an "ethic of risk" and then move on to analyze how decision making in fact unfolds. How this operates in a religious context, in cooperation with God's will, remains for a further section.

The distinction between an ethic of control and an ethic of risk was first posited by Sharon Welch.[16] Welch turns to the literature of African American women to elucidate the difference in moral agency between those with social and economic power and those on the margins. Her elucidation of these two ways of construing moral agency is relevant to our efforts to bring human actions within the purview of emergent probability.

An ethic of control assumes that moral agents can conceive of and execute actions with clear results. There is little room for ambiguity, for this ethic involves "controlling events and receiving a quick and predictable response."[17] With a clear plan, a decisive strategy, one is rendered invulnerable to the evil actions of others. The aim is to rid the world of the current evil and protect one from further threats. This view of moral action relies on "the equation of responsible action and control—the assumption that it is possible to guarantee the efficacy of one's actions."[18] Latent within this approach is the assumption of power, whereby one "defines action as the ability to attain, without substantial modification, desired results."[19] Though risk does not go unacknowledged in this perspective, it is merely considered as a variable to be managed.

Welch uses a character in Paule Marshall's novel *The Chosen Place, The Timeless People* to illustrate the often well-intentioned ethic of control. Harriet, a rich, white philanthropist, while working with the poor on a Caribbean island, comes upon two starving children in a meager hut. Harriet cannot bear the suffering of these hungry children, left alone while their parents are off cutting cane. Finding a half-dozen eggs in the hut, and in spite of the loud protests of the children, she breaks and scrambles the eggs over the fire. She is shocked later to discover that the eggs were meant for sale at the local market, that the children had been beaten for allowing her to cook them, and that, in fact, the children had left the cooked eggs untouched. Harriet had assumed that her quick, simple, and direct solution would solve the problem. She is out of touch with the complex systems of family and economic meaning in which she envisions herself acting as an agent of change.[20]

In contrast, an ethic of risk is "responsible action within the limits of bounded power" and involves "persistent defiance and resistance in the face of repeated defeats."[21] This ethic acknowledges action that may yield only partial results. The goal of moral action is not complete success but the creation of new conditions of possibility for the future. An ethic of risk accepts the long-term struggle involved in oppressive situations. It is "an ethic that begins with the recognition that we cannot guarantee decisive changes in the near future or even in our lifetime."[22] Further, "the ethic of risk is propelled by the equally vital recognition that to stop resisting, even when success is unimaginable, is to die," whether that involves physical death or the death of imagination and caring.[23]

Central to such situations is the engagement in a community of risk takers, committed to the struggle over the long haul. An ethic of risk involves strategic risk taking in the face of overwhelming odds, and recognizes the irreparable damage of structural evil.

Thus an ethic of control assumes that one's moral choices will "fix" evil in a definitive way, at times using force, coercion, or violence. It assumes a direct causality between action and its intended results. It is the preferred *modus operandi* of both oppressors and many well-intentioned charitable, religious, and political groups. An ethic of risk, however, recognizes the limits of power, the ambiguity of moral choice, and the partiality of any attempt to eradicate evil. It acknowledges that outcomes are often a matter of probabilities. Relying on the solidarity of community over the long haul, an ethic of risk looks more to creating a new matrix of possibilities rather than to finding a single direct solution to evil and its consequences.

Welch unpacks the notion of risk and control in light of the exercise of power. Hers is a social analysis that grounds a social ethic. While she speaks in terms of *prescriptive* norms, her notion of an ethic of risk has a *descriptive* element. By examining the way in which persons make value judgments and choices we discover that "risk" and "conditions of possibility" are inherent in moral action itself. We will thus move beyond Welch's work to outline the way we in fact go about making moral decisions. The first step involves an examination of how we know facts, but we then move on to the distinct aspects of value judgments and decisions.[24]

Coming to a conclusion that something is true depends on both coherence and empirical evidence. Questions arise, whether complex—What causes AIDS and which drugs are most effective in treating it?—or simple—What is that beeping sound that I hear? Proposed answers to these questions are accurate to the degree that they are internally consistent and, most important, match the evidence at hand. Now, the "evidence at hand" may come through simple perception, using our five senses, may rely on memory and previously attained knowledge, or may involve the collection of several layers of data via highly technical means. Either way, something is determined to be true, an explanation deemed correct, when the evidence sufficiently meets the conditions implicit in a proposed answer.

For example, the beeping sound is a French-fry machine *if:* (1) we are in the proximity of a fast-food restaurant; (2) the restaurant sells French fries; and (3) the restaurant uses a deep fryer that beeps when the French fries are done. If we are standing at a roadside fruit stand on a country road, then some other explanation, with its list of conditions, will need to be pursued. This simplistic model of determining the facts is repeated in much more elaborate forms in laboratories across the country. Much scholarly and scientific debate revolves around whether researchers have indeed verified their hypothetical claims with sufficient evidence.[25]

Making value judgments is a bit more complex. In decision making—both the mundane and the monumental—one determines not what *is* the case, but what *might be* the case. One weighs not the sufficiency of evidence to determine what is so, but projected courses of action and their potential outcomes. Surely, weighing these options depends a good deal on getting one's facts straight. If my car won't start, what I ought to do depends on what is wrong with it. Likewise, if I visit my mother and find her unconscious on the floor, my course of action must begin with at least a rudimentary determination of what has happened to her.

Nevertheless, judgments of value and decisions go beyond a mere determination of the current facts to a consideration of the probable outcomes of various courses of action. Thus, for example, once I get my mother to a hospital I seek expert advice about her condition. A resuscitation process has got her breathing regularly again, but it is unlikely that she will make it through the night without an artificial respirator. Intravenous medication may help her breathing but brings with it other side effects. No treatment at all, other than bed rest and vigilance from nursing staff, is also a possibility, but repeated resuscitation, if necessary, would further damage her fragile heart.

The point is that the choices involved here all include a consideration of direct causalities, on which one can rely with a great degree of certainty, and other outcomes that are subject to probabilities. Reliable schemes of recurrence (what drugs have what effects, all things being equal) combine with elements of "chance" (possible side effects that occur sometimes but not always) to inform our choices. With regard to the latter, the more accurate the predictions are, the more informed our choices can be. But no matter how accurate certain predictions are, probabilities never determine specific outcomes in concrete instances.

Recall that statistical science concerns itself with how often something is likely to occur, under which circumstances. It arrives at general conclusions that come in the form of averages and frequencies. One can take a survey of people who have used a certain drug treatment, determine how many have had which side effects, and then predict the likelihood of a new patient having the same side effects. But actual instances revolve randomly around an average. And the average, however accurately calculated, will not determine which actual instances will occur in the future.

Classical science helps us in decision making by elucidating causal relations, all other things being equal. As science advances—for example, in diagnosing diseases through genetic testing—our range of options can become more reliable. Statistical research can aid our choosing by indicating the relative probabilities of outcomes when statistical causality is involved. Nevertheless, no matter how simple or sophisticated one's considerations, no matter how rudimentary or elaborate one's predictions, the very *nature* of decision making will always involve the uncertainty of not knowing *exactly* what the concrete repercussions of one's actions will be. At some point one must make a decision and take action, accepting the risks involved in what might unfold.

There is a further element here, and that involves the weighing of values and the willingness of the agent. Once one has assessed the likelihood of certain outcomes to particular courses of action, one also weighs the relative values at stake in such various courses of action, as well as one's own level of commitment to such values. Thus, though the likelihood of my mother surviving is greater if I agree to have her put on a respirator, the quality of her life will be severely compromised. I must weigh her quality of life with the value of her physical survival. Perhaps my mother has previously indicated that she prefers a "good death," even if hastened by a lack of treatment. At the same time a respirator could easily prevent her from dying. All these considerations go well beyond the mere predictions of what will happen if I take various actions. *Given* these predictions I must still weigh the values involved, as well as my own willingness to carry out certain choices, and to live with the impending consequences.

Thus there is a deeper level of *existential risk* involved in value judgments and decisions. Beyond gathering information on probable outcomes, one must discern and weigh the relative values involved and consider one's willingness to accept responsibility for the consequences.

This existential risk is amply illustrated in Mildred Taylor's *Roll of Thunder, Hear My Cry.* Set in the southern United States during the Depression, Cassie Logan's Mama teaches the black children in their district and is committed to instilling dignity in her students and teaching them their own history. One day the white men of the local school board arrive unexpectedly to observe her teaching:

> Mama seemed startled to see the men, but when Mr. Granger said, "Been hearing 'bout your teaching, Mary, so as members of the school board we thought we'd come by and learn something," she merely nodded and went on with her lesson. . . . Mama was in the middle of

history and I knew that was bad. . . . But Mama did not flinch; she always started her history class the first thing in the morning when the students were most alert, and I knew that the hour was not yet up. To make matters worse, her lesson for the day was slavery. She spoke on the cruelty of it; of the rich economic cycle it generated as slaves produced the raw products for the factories of the North and Europe; how the country profited and grew from the free labor of a people still not free. Before she had finished, Mr. Granger picked up a student's book, flipped it open to the pasted-over front cover, and pursed his lips. . . . "I don't see all them things you're teaching in here."

"That's because they're not in there," Mama said.

"Well, if it ain't in here, then you got no right teaching it. This book's approved by the Board of Education and you're expected to teach what's in it."

"I can't do that."

"And why not?"

Mama, her back straight and her eyes fixed on the men, answered, "Because all that's in that book isn't true."

Mr. Granger stood. . . . "You must be some kind of smart, Mary. . . . In fact, . . . you're so smart I expect you'd best just forget about teaching altogether . . . then thataway you'll have plenty of time to write your own book."[26]

In this case the probability of a negative outcome, should Mama continue the lesson, is fairly high. Nevertheless, Mama chooses to continue because she decides that the value of maintaining her dignity, and that of the students, is more important than her job and safety. She chooses her own self-authenticity over the value of employment.

In sum, human moral agency involves us in various kinds of risk. There is the minor risk involved in getting our facts straight—we might be mistaken. There is the further risk inherent in decision making itself, which considers probable outcomes of various courses of action. While certain actions have fairly clear results, in many cases we are simply shifting probabilities in a matrix of complex relations and possible outcomes. Finally, there is the existential risk of establishing one's future and contributing to the character one becomes. This character will itself be the foundation of future choices, the underlying basis of further decisions.

The point thus far has been to indicate that in our decision making we rely on both "control" (reliable processes) and "risk" (probable outcomes). We have seen in previous chapters that the unfolding of nature is not merely a matter of direct causality, as in a Newtonian worldview, but involves contingencies—in other words, operates according to probabilities of events and systems of events occurring or not. So also human living involves both regular expectations and the consideration of likely outcomes when we make choices. We make some choices in which we can assume reliable outcomes—A causes B on a consistent basis. In addition to these instances there are many occasions when the outcomes of our actions occur according to schedules of probability. Thus our decisions involve relative levels of risk as we choose which courses to pursue.

HUMAN CONTROL VERSUS SHIFTING PROBABILITIES: EXAMPLES

The shift in worldview away from determinism includes a shift in how we conceive of our own actions. Many of us continue to think that a single action, strategy, or policy will directly cause a desired outcome. This has gone along with a failure to grasp interwoven systems of causality. In addition, we often assume that "man" is independent of "nature." Here we recount several examples of human interventions that have had systemic results. In the first two cases, human actions, rather than producing the single result envisioned, shifted ecological or evolutionary schemes of recurrence. In the third case, a few simple changes in a devastated community were able to increase the likelihood of new patterns of meaning and cooperation.

A first illustration comes from the history of wildlife management in the United States. In the early twentieth century the notion of "pristine nature" contributed to a naïveté about wilderness "preservation." Alston Chase, in his book *Playing God in Yellowstone*, recounts the efforts to protect the mule deer on the Kaibab peninsula, just north of the Grand Canyon, by establishing a game preserve:

> As part of the effort to protect the deer, all hunting was banned from the Kaibab, and predators were eliminated. In the first twenty-five years, government managers killed 4,889 coyotes, 781 mountain lions, 554 bobcats, and 20 wolves. Even more were killed by professional hunters hired by private stockmen.

As the government managers hoped, the deer began to increase. By 1918, the herd was estimated at 15,000 head.

But they succeeded too well. By 1923, estimates of the herd ranged from 30,000 to 100,000. With the increase in deer the range began to deteriorate. Favored browse species and shrubs disappeared as noxious plants spread. Gulleys—washouts—were appearing in the coulees; high-lining—stripping of the lower branches of trees—was evident; young trees, particularly aspen and Douglas fir, were killed . . .

By 1924 the herd crashed. The best estimates of those on the scene was that 60 percent of the herd died of starvation. This event was followed by a continuous, slow decline, as the decimated herd attempted to eke out a living on an impoverished range. Meanwhile the damage they did was enormous . . .

By the 1930s the Kaibab had become a textbook example of the perils of playing God. It was a story that greatly influenced the intellectual development of the great American conservationist (and author of *Sand County Almanac*) Aldo Leopold. Once a believer in killing wolves and lions to save deer, he had made a visit to the Kaibab in 1941, cementing a doubt that had been growing for decades: these animals, at the apex of the biotic pyramid, were not, as his contemporaries still thought, the "Nazis of the forest"; rather, they were the indispensable cornerstone for game management.[27]

As it turned out, the ideal of returning to a pristine wilderness incorporated a misguided assumption of control. The attempt to "fix" a problem in nature only led to massive destruction of both the herds and the ecosystem that sustained them.

The antibiotic war against human ailments reveals similar assumptions. Hospitals in the Western world began using antibiotics regularly in the 1950s. Today, one out of every three patients in a Western hospital is on antibiotics, but the resistance to these drugs is keeping pace, or even outpacing them. The battle against infectious disease has followed the same path as that of pesticide battles in agriculture: big companies, big medicine, and blanket treatment, followed by surprise at failure.[28] In an understated truth, biologist Martin Taylor comments: "It's generally the case that these chemical companies are not familiar with evolution."[29]

In fact, it is now the case that, in terms of contracting an untreatable infectious disease, the most dangerous place to be in a modernized country is a hospital. This is where the most sophisticated, most resistant, most elite bacteria now reside. Harold Neu of Columbia University insists that it is "critical for doctors, patients, and drug companies to avoid all unnecessary use of antibiotics, for humans or for animals, 'because this selective pressure has been what has brought us to this crisis.'"[30]

Thus we face the irony:

> Precisely where we wish to control the environment most tightly and possess it most completely we are powerless to do so, besieged and beleaguered by resistance movements that seem to spring up faster the more we lop them off. . . . The harder we fight these resistance movements, the harder and faster they evolve before our eyes—precisely because it is our effort at control that is driving their evolution. What we call control is to them merely a change in the environment, just another change in an endless series of changes.[31]

These two examples illustrate a misconstrued understanding of the relationship between humans and the nonhuman world, as well as the human assumption of control. *Homo sapiens*, it turns out, are not only products of but contributors to evolution. An alternative illustration reveals a recognition of the interaction of risk and control in transforming human relations.

Nicole Pageau is a woman from Edmonton, Canada, who in 2004 heard a widow from Rwanda talk about the effects the 1994 genocide was still having in that country.[32] Moved by this talk, Nicole, single and approaching age sixty, decided to move to Rwanda to see what she could do. She ended up in Kimironko, a village of seven hundred women and children who survived the massacre and were scrambling to make a living. These women include Karitas, a sixty-nine-year-old grandmother whose husband and all but one child were killed in the massacre. When she was taken by the Interehamwe herself, she expected to be murdered, but they left her alive, telling her they preferred to let her die of sadness. She now lives in poverty trying to raise two school-age grandsons. Another younger woman, Jeannette, was six months pregnant when the Hutu militia killed her husband and all but one son. Nine men raped her until she fainted and was left for dead in a pile of bodies, including her mother's. She now lives with the AIDS with which these men deliberately infected her. Not only are these women poor, they are traumatized and live lives of isolation and despair.

The Rwandan government had set aside a portion of its annual budget to help those recovering from the genocide. But the entire Rwandan annual budget was only around five hundred million dollars—equivalent to what a city like Toronto or Sydney spends each year on fire fighting and garbage collection. When Nicole arrived she had several thousand dollars that she and a friend had collected in Edmonton. She started by using the money to set up a food bank so that these women would not have to earn money through selling sex or begging. This was a beginning, but Nicole knew that she had to find ways for these women to earn money and to deal with their trauma. A breakthrough came when the women began making crafts with beads, which they sold to Nicole's supporters back in Edmonton and to local tourists. Nicole also found a few sponsors to cover the $100 a year it costs for children to go to school. Gradually, these sponsorships grew so that twenty-five children now attend school with supplies and uniforms that they otherwise could not have afforded.

One of the most important steps came when Nicole invited a nurse to come and talk to the women about trauma. No amount of food, or scholarships, or money would be able to eradicate the searing memories of the atrocities these women had undergone or had witnessed. The women listened intently to the nurse's presentation; at the end one woman asked: "Is there any cure for this trauma?" The nurse answered: "Yes, there is one and only one— you have to talk about it."

Shortly thereafter, a young woman came and asked Nicole if they could have a talk. Florid had been only twelve when the Interehamwe had destroyed her father's house and killed him. She herself fled to the jungle where she hid from the violence. At one point, with youthful bravado, she returned to the place she loved the most—her school. When she arrived the teacher asked her why she had come back. Why would she want to learn? When Florid answered that this was her school and this is where she belonged the teacher mocked her, telling her that there was no point in her learning, she wasn't even a human being. She would no doubt be killed soon anyway, so why bother learning? This was so demeaning to this young, impressionable girl that it seared her imagination. She told Nicole: "I just want to feel like a human being."

Eventually, Nicole managed to find some sewing machines for the women. This meant that they could sew uniforms for their children to go to school.

They then put in a bid for, and won, a contract to make all the uniforms for students at a nearby college. In just a few years, then, this village has become a haven of women who, out of despair, have found community and dignity. They not only have some income; they have a sense of contributing something, of doing work that is meaningful, of having a future for their children.

Nicole Pageau admits that she has not "fixed" anything. There is no utopian vision here, no surgical strike by which pain and poverty will be eradicated. Instead, Nicole and the widows together have established the "conditions for the possibility" for change. A food bank, a few sewing machines, crafts with beads, a small charity in Edmonton—all of these shifted the probabilities toward not only survival but *meaningful* survival. The risks that many have taken make it more likely that these women and their children will both live and die with dignity and a sense of hope.

Nicole Pageau's efforts have established new schemes of recurrence—regularities in which people can expect income, work, health care, and community on a stable basis. In fact, what has been established is some sense of *control*. The ethic of risk has yielded new conditions in which predictable patterns of both sustenance and meaning are available. Note, further, that just as important as regular schemes of sustenance and income are the patterns of cooperation that create meaning and community. Working together, sharing stories of trauma, these, too, are schemes of recurrence that have emerged and have established the possibility of meaning where there was none before.

These examples illustrate several things. First, we can continue to behave as if our actions create direct and simple results. But these actions usually backfire for, indeed, the outcomes of our actions are multiple, systemic, and subject to "chance." Alternatively, recognizing that outcomes are partial, systemic, and subject to probabilities, we can take small steps that gradually build into new schemes of recurrence. In so doing we don't fix situations definitively but set up new conditions of possibility for the transformation of both human and nonhuman communities.

GOD'S PROVIDENTIAL WILL, GRATEFUL COOPERATION, AND SACRIFICIAL LOVE

So what does God have to do with any of this? Throughout the book we have been making a case for a concept of God as transcendent yet nonetheless the author of the interaction of chance and necessity as the world unfolds. God is involved not as a secondary agent but as the primary cause of all that is, who has directed the dynamism of the world toward the good, ultimately the good of being in communion with God's self. We as human agents do serve as secondary causes, and because the world unfolds as an interaction of regularity and probability our actions involve the dialectic of control and risk. In fact, much as we wish it were otherwise, this is how it works. Our current situation consists of a complex set of schemes of recurrence and our attempts to change it will necessarily shift conditions according to the relative probabilities involved.

Now, the ethic of control as outlined by Sharon Welch leans in the direction of power and hubris. Indeed, it is often the case that those with economic or cultural power are able more easily to presume the direct causality of control. Likewise, those who are more vulnerable tend to be aware of the vicissitudes of life and to realize that their choices merely shift a situation incrementally. They are often those whose actions put them in the position of taking risks. But as we have seen in Rwanda, the regularity of social schemes of recurrence is conducive to healthy communities: control can be an important aspect of healthy living.

At the same time, the mere recognition of probability in calculating the results of our choices does not necessarily make one humble. Indeed, investment bankers and military strategists "manage" risk all the time. Consideration of risk—taking stock of probability outcomes—can be in the service of hubris, oppression, self-indulgence.

This is where a recognition of a Creator upon whom all of existence depends can place the entire dialectic of chance and necessity, risk and control in another perspective. If indeed we are not responsible for our own existence, if we accept our role as creatures and forswear our attempts to be godlike, we begin to see that all we have is a matter of gift. In the finite arena in which we are responsible for the future or can make changes, we accept that the meager resources we have are not our own creations to exploit.

Thus the ethic of control and the ethic of risk need to be complemented with an ethic of gratitude. Surely belief in a Creator God is an act of faith that not all will make. But we have indicated that at least the question "Why is there something rather than nothing?" can lead reasonably to the notion of a Source of all that is who is not a creature made by yet something else. And if this is a reasonable position, the implications for our own self-conception follow: we are creatures, our existence is given to us, and we are responsible for what we make of ourselves. An ethic of gratitude is thus grounded in an acknowledgment of both a Creator and our creaturely dependence.

Our sense of responsibility, our moral agency, thus can take on a new tenor. In an attitude of thanks for our existence we move beyond merely a calculation of risk or presumption of control to seeking to promote God's provident will in the world. While God knows all that is and will be in a single act, we do not. Living in space and time we yet need to create our futures without knowing exactly what impact we might have. Nevertheless, we can choose to create conditions by which we become more sensitive to God's loving action. We can tune ourselves to the needs of others, especially the marginalized and victimized. We can develop an intentional relationship with God in an effort to be more attentive, intelligent, reasonable, and responsible about how we live.

The practices by which we seek to understand what God is up to in our part of the world are practices of discernment. Such discernment and the habits that foster them become psychological and spiritual patterns that are foundational schemes of recurrence on which character choices are built. Over time one can become more and more adept at discerning the right thing to do given the circumstances at hand. Furthermore, communities of discernment, committed to fostering loving relationships in community, can create a tradition whereby wisdom is passed on. A heritage of both spiritual practices and moral habits comes to be taken for granted, heightening the likelihood (though not the certainty) that younger generations will have the tools they need to develop healthy relationships with God and others.[33]

Now, just as evolution includes failures and breakdowns as well as newly emergent possibilities, so, too, at the human level choices of individuals and of groups can work against the upwardly directed dynamism of finality. Questions about the facts of a case can be ignored or obscured. Self-transcendent values can be replaced with selfishness. Groups can impose a bias that refuses to consider all the relevant aspects of a situation. Prejudice can be inherited so that younger generations are not given opportunities even to rub shoulders with those designated as tainted or deviant. The failure to be attentive, intelligent, reasonable, and responsible that is at the heart of evil yields consequences that even renewed reason cannot sort out. In the end we have situations that embody the "surd"—the lack of intelligibility at the heart of systemic evils—making situations irrational and saturated with moral impotence.

Thus the practical reorientation of cycles of evil gets complex indeed. Reversing the consequences of moral evil is not a matter of direct causality. Not only does the ethic of control offer an incorrect assessment of moral agency, assumptions that executing plan A so that evil B will be eradicated can serve to continue the systems that were problematic in the first place. Indeed, it is precisely this kind of deterministic presumption that tends to perpetuate cycles of violence, oppression, addiction, and abuse. Victims try to alleviate their pain by wiping out the perceived source of their victimization. This in turn merely creates more victims who then become perpetrators of further violence, addiction, or abuse. Since evil has at its base no reason for being, in fact it is the absence of being, the intuition that things can be righted if only we get back to the basic error and put right the scales is inevitably wrong.

In the end, the solution to putting right a system in which irrational evil is embedded is not direct "eradication" but the replacement of irrationality with reason, the offering of love in the face of degradation, providing meaning where only despair has been. The solution to the problem of evil becomes not justice, mistaken as revenge, but mercy, forgiveness, and sacrificial love. The reorientation this allows builds a new reality, a new set of meanings, that makes up for the "reason" that was lacking before.

So we come full circle to Gandhi, Mama, Nicole and the women of Kimironko, and, of course, Jesus. To stand up for reason in the face of the irrational, to claim dignity and justice in spite of oppression and degradation, these are dangerous options in tenuous and fragile circumstances. And often the forces against which one acts react with more violence and demeaning behavior. In spite of his message of love, Jesus was crucified. Mama spoke the truth but lost her job. Gandhi exposed the injustice of British colonialism and was assassinated. But these acts of sacrificial love became, in turn, the conditions of possibility for transformation. Mama and her students could hold their heads high and stand up with pride. In the end, the British colonial powers had to succumb to the claims of the people of India. The sacrifices that Nicole and her Canadian group made set the conditions of possibility for these women survivors to tell their stories, not eliminate the wounds, but retell what had happened and remake their lives with purpose. And, finally, Jesus' followers went into all the world in joy and strength convinced that God's power encompasses and heals even the worst and darkest moments of history.

CONCLUSION

In this chapter we have highlighted both the ordinary evolution of and the uniqueness of *Homo sapiens*. While our species has emerged along with all other life through the interaction of chance and necessity over many thousands of generations, we remain distinctive in our use of symbolic language, our technology, culture, and self-reflection. The work of the Leakeys and that of genetic researchers illustrate the great advances of knowledge that can take place when we use our innate curiosity to pursue questions of the unknown. A new level of spiritual orientation to meaning and value has emerged: in this sense we are "made in the image of God."

At the same time, our understanding of the world has been shifting from the determinism of Newtonian science to the consideration of chance as it unfolds along with the regularities studied by classical science. These considerations apply to our uniquely human capabilities as much as they do to the emergent probability of nonhuman species. Even our own moral agency, as it turns out, involves the uncertainty of probable outcomes along with the relative assurance of regular patterns of recurrence. So we live with both an "ethic of control" as well as an "ethic of risk." To assume that we have control—that our actions will result in simple and direct outcome—is not only erroneous but can verge on the imperialistic.

If we live within the purview of a religious worldview that acknowledges a Creator and recognizes the vast dependence of all creation on that Creator, both an ethic of risk and an ethic of control can be subsumed within an ethic of gratitude. In this case, trying to make good decisions includes habits of discernment, most often embedded in communities of discernment, in an effort to grasp and cooperate with God's providential will. Finally, such efforts may lead us into the conundrum of the irrationality of evil and its consequences. And the restoring of right relations comes often not from direct causality but from the self-sacrificing love that restores relations in spite of wrongs done, the transformation of lives that can emerge out of and in spite of the complete failure of moral agency to do the right thing. Indeed, such restoration as a fruit of self-sacrificial love, mercy, and forgiveness is at the very heart of God's provident will for the whole.

CONCLUSION

CAN A TRANSCENDENT GOD BE A PERSONAL GOD?

Throughout this work we have argued that the classical account of God as transcendent—for example, eternal, omnipotent, and omniscient—is not only compatible with an evolving world order and the findings of modern cosmology, but in fact presents a more coherent response to the challenges modern science poses than alternative accounts that seek to make God subject to change. There remains an enduring challenge, however, not from science but from those who argue that the transcendent God of classical theism is simply not compatible with the God of the Bible, a personal God who loves us, who acts to save us, and with whom we can have a personal relationship.[1] In the Bible we find a God who is passionate about human beings, who responds to the prayers of God's faithful ones. The transcendent God, on the other hand, is perceived as remote, removed from God's creation, cold and uncaring. This is the question we seek to address in this conclusion. Is the transcendent God of classical theism a God we can pray to, with whom we can enter into a personal relationship, a God who loves and cares for us?

Throughout the book we have challenged the "picture thinking" that humans often engage in when thinking about God and creation. At the most basic level we have argued against the tendency to think of God as just like us, only much, much bigger and much, much older. We have used analytic language and discursive reasoning to promote our positions. But we need to emphasize, as we come to the conclusion of our work, that such explanatory categories and the precision that comes with them, while important, are not the only ways to talk about God. In fact, metaphoric, poetic, narrative language is not only important but necessary in talking about God. Precisely because God is so far "beyond" what we can conceive—indeed, because terms such as "vast" or "outside space and time" themselves break down when we urge a robust transcendent view of God—we will continually strive to find metaphors and images that will adequately push us past our narrow conceptions. Story telling, analogies, poetic juxtaposition, liturgical practice, symbolic rituals: all of these will perdure as we struggle both to relate to God and yet to make sure that our God is not too small. As we come to the end of our work, then, we explore how the grand vision we have asserted of God and creation squares with our lived relationship with such a transcendent God.

Let us begin by reviewing what we have argued in the earlier chapters. In agreement with modern science (evolution, quantum mechanics) we can acknowledge genuine chance operating on the cosmos. Drawing on the work of Bernard Lonergan we have presented a world with both deterministic classical laws and nondeterministic statistical laws, which interact to produce a world order of emergent probability, illustrated with various examples drawn from different branches of science.[2] Moreover, when we take into account Einstein's theories of relativity (special and general), we have to acknowledge the interrelationship of time and space. Far from living in a three-dimensional space with an independent temporal dimension, Einstein has taught us to think in terms of a four-dimensional space-time where space and time are relative to observers, and no observer is privileged in terms of defining coordinates of space and time. One consequence of his theories is that there is no well-defined cosmic notion of "now." Two observers moving relative to one another cannot agree as to what constitutes "now."[3] From this perspective, the assumption that God knows what is happening "now" but not what will happen in the "future" is problematic, because there is no well-defined concept of "now." Contemporary cosmology reinforces this by arguing that time is inextricable from creation itself. If time is inextricable from creation, God's being must exist outside time.[4]

These scientific perspectives agree very well with the account given by classical theism. In that account God is a primary cause of being, bringing everything, space and time, or more correctly space-time, into existence. What science uncovers in terms of classical and statistical laws are what that tradition refers to as secondary causes. These are genuine causes—gravity does cause objects to fall (classical); smoking does cause lung cancer (statistical)—but they do not explain existence itself, including the existence of such classical and statistical laws. God is the cause of their existence and, indeed, the existence of everything that exists or occurs. To repeat the words of Martin Rees, "Theorists may, some day, be able to write down fundamental equations governing physical reality. But physics can never explain what 'breathes fire' into the equations, and actualizes them in a real cosmos."[5] God is the cause of being, the one who breathes fire into the equations to make a real cosmos.

Still, we are left with a God who is "outside" space and time. And so we can ask, How can such a God be "close" to us? Before we attempt to answer this question, we should pause for a moment and consider the imagery behind it. The question itself is posed in spatio-temporal terms. To be close to us, someone must be physically in the same location as ourselves; when someone is far away, it is more difficult to think of them as "close." Almost by necessity, a God who is not part of space and time cannot then be "close" to us.

Now let us turn the question around. What if we were to ask not how is God close to us, but how are we close to God? As we have argued throughout, God is the one who creates us. This act of creation is not some impersonal act of a blind force of nature, nor something God is compelled to do out of some type of inner necessity, but an act of loving wisdom and wise loving. God knows us through and through because God's loving wisdom is cause of all that is; and God's wise loving freely chooses us and everything else in this cosmos from all other possible universes. God literally knows and loves us into existence. As such, we are intimately close to God; not the closeness of a physical proximity, but the closeness of knowing and loving, an intimacy that causes us to be. We truly are "written in the palm of God's hand."

And of course we are not just talking about the "Big Bang," or our conception, or any other particular initial event in space and time. Every moment, every location, every event, every being during all its existence is known and loved into that existence by God. Of course, we have already discussed the problem of evil, and the nature of evil as "nonbeing," but one consequence of the classical view of God is that there is no situation, no matter how desperate, no matter how dark, where evil threatens to overwhelm us; there is no situation in which God is not active in seeking to redeem that situation.

Indeed, this relationship of Creator to creature, of God to us, is so unconditional, so absolute, that even when we fall into the nonbeing of sin, God does not desert us, does not cease knowing and loving us into being. We, too, are secondary causes in our own right; we decide and act, and God supports the existence of this real form of causation even when we act sinfully. As we have discussed earlier, this does not make God responsible for the evil, but it does demonstrate the unconditional love that God has for us even in our sinning. For God maintains us in existence even when we sin.

Do we then make a difference to God? Does it make sense to pray to God? Does prayer change anything? If God is eternally the same, unchanging and independent of time, then does that not make God unresponsive? Again, this is the type of criticism often made toward classical theism. Of course, there are pastoral things that can be said about how prayer changes us, making us more attuned to others and ourselves and so more able to deal with difficulties and challenges. But this does not seem to have an impact in any way on God. Again, if we examine the image behind this, we find an image of a God who needs to be stirred into action, to be awoken from a divine slumber to act, in order to do what needs to be done. What if, instead, classical theism presents us with a God who is infinitely responsive, who has responded so fully and so completely in the one divine act of creation that no further response is possible or needed?[6] In the one infinite act of creation, past, present, and future *for us*, God responds to all our prayers and petitions, answers all our needs, all guided by an infinite divine loving wisdom and wise loving. This is the notion of divine providence that we explored in chapter 5. And while God's response *to us* is itself eternal and unchanging, it unfolds *for us* in the fullness of time. Thus God responds to this prayer in our here and now. And if we do not pray, God does not so respond. Prayer is meaningful, it does change the situation, and God does act in response to our prayers. But this does not amount to some intervention along the lines of stirring an inactive God into action, but is part of the one creative act of God who brings into existence everything that is.

This same observation can be made in relation to Christian belief in the incarnation. Without going into the trinitarian aspects of this belief, which would move us well into fundamentally distinctive Christian beliefs and beyond the scope of this book, one can ask whether classical theism can conceive of such a possibility. Does not the incarnation by its very nature involve God in the temporal order and imply a divine intervention into the created order? Of course, it is very easy to read the incarnation in a mythological way, something like the way in which Greek or Roman gods would take on human form in order to engage in various activities in the world (often of a salacious nature). Christianity has always resisted such an understanding of the incarnation in its doctrinal formulations, however much alive that mythological understanding may be in popular imagination. In the formulation of the Council of Chalcedon (451 CE), the two natures, divine and human, remain distinct, ensuring that the transcendence of the divine nature is ensured.[7] While we may struggle with the distinction the council introduces between person and nature, it clearly intended to maintain the transcendence of the divine nature, while allowing the divine person of the Son to be fully incarnate in a human nature. On the one hand, the existence of this divine person in a human nature is temporal, finite, material, and capable of suffering. The divine nature, on the other hand, remains eternal, infinite, spiritual, and incapable of suffering. How this may be so takes us beyond the immediate concerns of this work, though it remains a profound theological issue.

As to the question of the incarnation being an "intervention," we can note that the same position above in relation to prayer holds in terms of the incarnation. The incarnation is known and willed eternally by God, but occurs in space and time. It is not a change in God acting, but a manifestation in time of God's eternal creative activity. In this way it is not a question of God moving from inactivity to activity, of intervening where before God was not active, but of God's eternal activity being manifest in a spatio-temporal manner.

And so we would claim that the transcendent God can be a personal God, a God who responds to our prayers, who can even enter into human history in an incarnation. Such a God is congruent not only with scientific expectation, but with our religious sensibilities. But is the effort to maintain such a rigorous classical theism worth the effort? Why not simply adopt the position promoted by some, that God can and must change as the world changes, that God cannot and does not know the future any more than we can, and that God can be surprised by genuine novelty in the world? Is not this a more "human" god?

Just as such a stance has interrogated classical theism, so, too, we can ask pointed questions in response. Could a god who can change be diminished? Could such a god be weakened, particularly in the face of evil? Can we be assured that a changing god will be able to deal with the problem of evil? Perhaps such a god could be overcome by the problem of evil, diminished to the point of ineffectiveness? Can such a god love us unconditionally? And can we be assured that such a god would not change that god's stance in relation to us, to turn from love to hate or indifference? Why should we rule out these types of changes in God as well? And what of the goodness of creation? If all creation is not the product of divine wisdom and love, because God, too, is surprised by novelty in creation, can we be assured that creation is "very good"? If so, there must be some source of goodness other than God. Either that or the goodness of creation is compromised and we risk falling over into dualism. In the end, is such a god worthy of our love and worship, or simply too much made in our image and likeness?

Certainly the God of classical theism is mysterious. The divine existence is not like our own, not just a larger version of ourselves. We can only get a glimpse of what this existence might be like, such as a blinding moment of insight, or the complacent serenity of being loved and in love, timeless experiences where everything else both stands still and falls into place. This is the God in whom we can take eternal delight because this God is the source of all novelty, all meaning, all truth, all beauty, and all love, inexhaustibly mysterious and wonderful.

NOTES

CHAPTER 1. GOD, RELIGION, AND SCIENCE

1. There is evidence that heliocentric models such as those developed by Copernicus were developed in the East prior to his work.

2. Metaphysics is the branch of philosophy that is concerned with the fundamental nature of all reality (that which is "beyond" [*meta*] physics). A metaphysical view of the world incorporates explicit or implicit assumptions about what constitutes reality itself—e.g., that only matter is real and intangibles such as spirit, mind, feelings are mere illusions. Every era and culture embodies such assumptions, whether explicitly acknowledged or not. Many of the current debates over science and religion, for example, are not about science or religion as much as they are about metaphysical assumptions underpinning these enterprises. See http://www.philosophypages.com/dy/m7.htm#mephy.

3. There was a dispute between Newton and another mathematician, Gottfried Wilhelm Leibnitz (1646–1716), over who actually invented calculus. In his *Principia mathematica* Newton deliberately hid his invention behind a purely geometrical approach, whereas Leibnitz published his discoveries and so was initially credited with them.

4. Newton's own religious beliefs tended toward Unitarianism, that is, a nontrinitarian belief in God. See Stephen Snobelen, "Isaac Newton, Heretic: The Strategies of a Nicodemite," *British Journal of the History of Science* 32 (1999): 381–419. He also dabbled in alchemy.

5. Isaac Newton, *Principia mathematica,* concluding "General Scholium."

6. Michael J. Behe, *Darwin's Black Box: The Biochemical Challenge to Evolution*, 10th ann. ed. (New York: Free, 2006); idem, *The Edge of Evolution: The Search for the Limits of Darwinism* (New York: Free, 2007); William A. Dembski, *Intelligent Design: The Bridge between Science and Theology* (Downers Grove, IL: InterVarsity, 1999); idem, *The Design Revolution: Answering the Toughest Questions About Intelligent Design* (Downers Grove, IL: InterVarsity, 2004); idem and Sean McDowell, *Understanding Intelligent Design* (Eugene, OR: Harvest House, 2008).

7. Michael Buckley argues that Deism is a major factor in the rise of modern atheism; see his *At the Origins of Modern Atheism* (New Haven: Yale University Press, 1987).

8. This excerpt from Augustine was quoted by Galileo in his defense of his account of the solar system; see http://history.hanover.edu/courses/excerpts/111gal2.html. The second image, of the heavens as a dish that "covers and overcasts the earth," is what a literal reading of Genesis 1 would require. It is doubtful that any Christian fundamentalist would accept this as a scientific statement.

9. Erich Wasmann, "Catholics and Evolution," in *The Catholic Encyclopedia*, vol. 5 (New York: Robert Appleton, 1909), available at http://www.newadvent.org/cathen/05654a.htm.

10. Jacques Monod, *Chance and Necessity: An Essay on the Natural Philosophy of Modern Biology* (New York: Vintage, 1972).

11. Particularly in Richard Dawkins, *The Blind Watchmaker: Why the Evidence of Evolution Reveals a Universe without Design* (New York: Norton, 1996).

12. Charles Hartshorne, *Aquinas to Whitehead: Seven Centuries of Metaphysics of Religion* (Milwaukee: Marquette University Press, 1976); Ian G. Barbour, *When Science Meets Religion* (San Francisco: HarperSanFrancisco, 2000).

13. The proposal was jointly developed by Einstein, Boris Podolsky, and Nathan Rosen.

14. David Bohm, *Wholeness and the Implicate Order*, Routledge Classics (London: Routledge, 2002).

15. Dawkins, *Blind Watchmaker*, 5; emphasis in the original.

16. In fact, the dichotomy between chance and design is evident in the title of Christopher Schönborn, *Chance or Purpose? Creation, Evolution, and a Rational Faith*, trans. Henry Taylor (San Francisco: Ignatius, 2007). Schönborn makes repeated references to the supposed dichotomy in his text. Similarly Behe, *Edge of Evolution*.

17. Richard Dawkins, *The God Delusion* (Boston: Houghton Mifflin, 2006), 214–22.

18. Ibid., 264.

19. Charles Taylor, *Sources of the Self: The Making of the Modern Identity* (Cambridge: Harvard University Press, 1989).

20. Sometimes this is described as a conflict between deductive and inductive methods. This is inaccurate. While Kepler used empirical calculations to discover that the orbits of the planets were elliptical (an inductive approach), it was Newton's deduction of elliptical orbits from mathematical formulation that made the results truly scientific and not just an unexplained observation.

21. Paul Davies's works include *The Edge of Infinity: Where the Universe Came from and How It Will End* (New York: Simon & Schuster, 1981); *God and the New Physics* (New York: Simon & Schuster, 1983); *The Last Three Minutes: Conjectures about the Ultimate Fate of the Universe*, Science Masters (New York: Basic, 1994); *The Mind of God: The Scientific Basis for a Rational World* (New York: Simon & Schuster, 2005); *The Goldilocks Enigma: Why Is the Universe Just Right for Life?* (London: Allen Lane, 2006).

22. Dawkins, *Blind Watchmaker*; idem, *God Delusion*.

23. Dawkins, *God Delusion*, 19.

24. Paul Davies, "Now Is the Reason for Our Discontent," *Sydney Morning Herald*, 1 January 2003.

25. Ibid. Weinberg's dictum is "The more the universe seems comprehensible the more it also seems pointless." Davies basically repeats his argument in *Goldilocks Enigma*, 17–18.

26. As Aquinas notes: "For when anyone in the endeavor to prove the faith brings forward reasons which are not cogent, he falls under the ridicule of the unbelievers: since they suppose that we stand upon such reasons, and that we believe on such grounds" *Summa Theologica* 1 q32 a1; see http://www.newadvent.org/summa/1032.htm.

27. For example, the two works by Alister E. McGrath: *Dawkins' God: Genes, Memes, and the Meaning of Life* (Malden, MA: Blackwell, 2005); idem and Joanna McGrath, *The Dawkins Delusion: Atheist Fundamentalism and the Denial of the Divine* (Downers Grove, IL: InterVarsity, 2007).

28. See Dawkins's article "The Improbability of God," *Free Inquiry* 18, no. 3 (1998), at http://www.secularhumanism.org/library/fi/dawkins_18_3.html. Contrary to Dawkins's assertions, the argument from design was not the major argument put forward traditionally. It only became the major argument in a more scientifically aware age, when metaphysics was on the wane.

29. In a sense this is a work in "natural theology," though one colored by an engagement with the Christian intellectual tradition. It is a natural theology in the Christian tradition without thereby being a Christian natural theology.

30. Bernard J. F. Lonergan, *Insight: A Study of Human Understanding*, ed. Frederick E. Crowe and Robert M. Doran, Collected Works of Bernard Lonergan, vol. 3 (Toronto: University of Toronto Press, 1992).

CHAPTER 2. EVOLVING WORLD: REGULARITY AND PROBABILITY

1. Paul Davies, "E.T. and God: Could Earthly Religions Survive the Discovery of Life Elsewhere in the Universe?," *The Atlantic Monthly* (September 2003), 112–18.

2. Ibid., 114. Davies is quoting Jacques Monod, *Chance and Necessity: An Essay on the Natural Philosophy of Modern Biology* (New York: Vintage, 1972), 180. See also Ian Barbour's use of this quote, and discussion, in his *Religion and Science: The Historical and Contemporary Issues* (San Francisco: HarperCollins, 1997), 79–80.

3. Davies, "E.T. and God," 114.

4. Ibid.

5. Charles Darwin, *On the Origin of Species by Means of Natural Selection* (Mineola, NY: Dover Publications, 2006 [1859]).

6. Your stockbroker will warn you: "Past performance is no indicator of future outcomes." In doing this he or she is alluding to the fact that actual performance does not always follow from past averages, and that particular instances (actual frequencies) do not always match averages over time (ideal frequencies).

7. One can distinguish between statistical work in which one knows the ideal frequency in advance (a priori), as in the coin-tossing or dice-rolling examples, and studies that involve an "after the fact" (a posteriori) counting of events. The first involve primarily mathematical calculations, while the latter involve "field work"—defining an event and setting parameters (usually time and place) in which to count these selected events. Note that in this latter case the accuracy of defining the events to be observed and the clear demarcation of the parameters within which these events will be counted is crucial for the usefulness and accuracy of the conclusions one will draw.

8. Note that this characteristic of statistical science means that the statistician is ever refining her findings. As the state of various aspects of the world changes, statisticians need to solicit new data and calculate new probabilities. This does not mean that statisticians never come to confident conclusions. They may be very accurate in their discovery of the state of something given the parameters set for their inquiry. But such states and the conditions underlying them may change. The only way to determine if they have changed is to do further, updated studies.

9. This kind of insight—that, in fact, there is no direct insight to be had—is what Lonergan calls an "inverse insight." See Bernard J. F. Lonergan, *Insight: A Study of Human Understanding*, ed. Frederick E. Crowe and Robert M. Doran, Collected Works of Bernard Lonergan, vol. 3 (Toronto: University of Toronto Press, 1992), 43–50, 78–81.

10. These examples are taken from Kenneth R. Melchin, *History, Ethics, and Emergent Probability: Ethics, Society, and History in the Work of Bernard Lonergan*, 2d ed. (Ottawa: Lonergan Web Site, 1999), 79ff; http://www.loneonerganresource.com/book.php?6. He adapts them from Philip McShane, *Randomness, Statistics, and Emergence* (Dublin: Gill & Macmillan, 1970), 71–76, who in turn takes them from J. L. Harper and G. R. Sager, "Some Aspects of the Ecology of Buttercups in Permanent Grassland," *Procedures of the British Weed Control Conference* 1 (1953): 256–63. Note that the figures used in the graph are entirely fictitious, created by the authors of this book for illustrative purposes.

11. Note that they would most likely do this using a sampling procedure (rather than counting every single buttercup plant). Such sampling itself is subject to the canons of statistical science.

12. The work of the Grants is recounted in Jonathan Weiner, *The Beak of the Finch* (New York: Vintage, 1995); see esp. chs. 3 and 4.

13. When Peter Grant began this work he was teaching at McGill University in Montreal. It was with the help of an engineer at McGill that he devised the "McGill nutcracker," which allowed the measurement of the difficulty of cracking different kinds of seeds, and, hence, the development of a "struggle index." See ibid, 56–57.

14. Note that each data point in this graph, and in tables 2.3, 2.4, and 2.5, represent *averages*. In other words, the data points do not represent single birds eating single seeds, but the average seed toughness eaten by birds with an average beak size. Note also that these tables are schematizations; the data points are fictional and illustrative only.

15. See Weiner, *Beak*, 58.

16. Ibid., 85.

17. We are indebted to Patrick Byrne of Boston College for both this example and his help in understanding these issues.

18. See Weiner, *Beak*, 78.

19. If some pattern were to occur in these actual cases, some other, systematic explanation would need to be sought, as illustrated above in the work of Trevor Price with young finches.

20. There is a further question that can be asked, which has to do with the extent of deviation from the norm in a given population. In the Galapagos, the Grant team found that the chance of finding a cactus finch with a beak 10 percent from the mean is four in a hundred. With regard to the depth of the upper mandible of the medium ground finch,

the probability of finding a 10 percent deviation is one in three. In contrast, among song sparrows on the island of Mandarte in British Columbia, there is much less variation. The chance of finding a bird with a beak that deviates 10 percent from the mean is only four in ten thousand. In this case, having determined average beak size in different populations, one is comparing populations to determine relative variability from the mean among populations. Clearly, the variability among song sparrows in British Columbia is much less than that of Darwin's finches. This variability is an essential component of evolution, whereby the more variability in a population the more likely it is to be subject to natural selection. See Weiner, *Beak*, 47.

21. Patrick Byrne, "Quaestio Disputata: Evolution, Randomness, and Divine Purpose: A Reply to Cardinal Schönborn," *Theological Studies* 67 (2006): 653–65, at 658. Byrne here refers to Karl Popper, *The Logic of Scientific Discovery* (New York: Harper & Row, 1959), 189–205. For a fuller discussion, see Patrick Byrne, "Lonergan, Evolutionary Science, and Intelligent Design," *Revista Portuguesa de Filosofia* 63 (2007): 893–913.

22. Lonergan's technical definition of emergent probability is "the successive realization in accord with successive schedules of probability of a conditioned series of schemes of recurrence" (Lonergan, *Insight*, 148–49). For a fuller explanation, see 138–62.

23. On schemes of recurrence, see ibid., 140–43.

24. Two ideas emerging in the scientific literature reflect this idea of schemes of recurrence. These are *autopoiesis* and *autocatalysis*. On the former, see http://pespmc1.vub.ac.be/ASC/AUTOPOIESIS.html. On the latter, see R. E. Ulanowicz, *Ecology: The Ascendent Perspective* (New York: Columbia University Press, 1997).

25. Global warming provides a most pertinent and publicly discussed example of the interlocking sets of schemes of recurrence in the natural world today.

26. Image taken from http://www.personal.kent.edu/~cearley/PChem/Krebs1.gif. Copyright © 2008 Clarke Earley, used with the permission of the author.

27. One could say that this unified whole is a *formal* cause, providing a (dynamic) form, unity, or essence that did not exist previously. This model of world process speaks against materialism and reductionism.

28. The image of a pyramid, of course, raises the question of "hierarchy" in the natural world, an idea that lost favor along with earlier notions of teleology and the demise of the "great chain of being." The notion that increased complexity represents a "higher" form of life is becoming more acceptable in scientific circles. See Ernst Mayr, *What Evolution Is* (New York: Basic, 2001), 278. David J. Depew and Bruce H. Weber conclude their long history and analysis of Darwinism by asserting that "'hierarchy talk' is no longer scandalous" (Depew and Weber, *Darwinism Evolving: Systems Dynamics and the Genealogy of Natural Selection* (Cambridge: MIT Press, 1995), 495. These are issues we will take up again in ch. 4.

29. See the story of how drought, and then severe rains, affected finch life on the island of Daphne Major in the Galapagos, in Weiner, *Beak*, chs. 4–7.

30. See Lonergan, *Insight*, 143–44. The point is that probabilities increase in incremental patterns, so Hoyle's analogy about the (low) likelihood of a whirlwind creating a Boeing 747 by blowing through a junkyard is misplaced. There are gradual increases in probabilities that make the creation of a Boeing 747 from junk more and more possible

over time. At the same time, such emergent schemes set limits to the direction of further developments. Such is the nature of "differentiation" of species over time.

31. Francisco J. Ayala, "Intelligent Design: The Original Version," *Theology and Science* 1 (2003): 9–32, at 20.

32. Ibid.

33. In other words, they calculate the probabilities by assuming independence and thus *multiplying* presumed probabilities with each other. As we have seen above, once a scheme of recurrence emerges, such that the incidence of one event ensures the occurrence of another event, probabilities leap substantially. This is essentially David J. Bartholomew's argument in his *God, Chance, and Purpose: Can God Have It Both Ways?* (Cambridge: Cambridge University Press, 2008); see esp. chs. 5 and 6.

34. The phrase "survival of the fittest," which is so often used to depict Darwin's theory of natural selection, was not actually invented by Darwin. It was coined, rather, by his friend and advocate Herbert Spencer, and was often used by Spencer to promote causes well beyond Darwin's intentions. See http://plato.stanford.edu/entries/spencer/.

35. Note, also, that there are two aspects of natural selection. One is the survival of those most adapted to their environments, but there is also the element of sexual selection. In order for natural selection to work over time, the beneficial adaptations that occur must be passed on to the next generation. Among other things, this means that those who are the most adapted to their environments must live to the age of reproduction and mate successfully. There are, then, also adaptive traits that make individuals more attractive to the opposite sex, so that adaptive traits are not only about those that enable survival but also those that enhance the chances of mating. See Weiner, *Beak*, 80–81, 85–96.

36. Ibid., 85. Emphasis added.

37. See http://evolution.berkeley.edu/evosite/evo101/IIIBMechanismsofchange.shtml.

38. Francisco J. Ayala, *Darwin and Intelligent Design*, Facets (Minneapolis: Fortress Press, 2006), 62ff.

39. Ibid., 63–64. Ayala is here is responding to arguments by intelligent-design advocates that the emergence of complexity is impossible through chance operations.

40. Note that natural selection does not *necessarily* lead to increasing complexity. See ibid., 65.

41. See Ernst Mayr's discussion of precisely this point in *Evolution*, 228–29. See also Ayala, "Intelligent Design," 24.

42. Byrne, "Evolution, Randomness, and Divine Purpose," 659. He goes on to note that this does not mean that the survival of these genetic variations is not subject to environmental conditions.

43. Mayr, *Evolution*, 120.

1. Charles Hartshorne, *Aquinas to Whitehead: Seven Centuries of Metaphysics of Religion* (Milwaukee: Marquette University Press, 1976), 15.

2. Bruce Epperly, *Process Theology: A Guide for the Perplexed* (New York: T & T Clark, 2011), vii. For other introductions to process theology, see John B. Cobb and David Ray

Griffin, *Process Theology: An Introductory Exposition* (Philadelphia: Westminster, 1976), and C. Robert Mesle, *Process Theology: A Basic Introduction* (St. Louis: Chalice, 1993).

3. Elizabeth A. Johnson, "Does God Play Dice? Divine Providence and Chance," *Theological Studies* 57 (1996): 10.

4. Joseph A. Bracken, "Response to Elizabeth Johnson's 'Does God Play Dice?'" *Theological Studies* 57 (1996): 720–30, at 724.

5. Ibid., 725–26.

6. Ibid., 729–30.

7. Alfred North Whitehead, *Process and Reality: An Essay in Cosmology*, ed. David Ray Griffin and Donald W. Sherburne (New York: Free, 1978), 348.

8. Bernard McGinn, "The Development of the Thought of Thomas Aquinas on the Reconciliation of Divine Providence and Contingent Action," *Thomist* 39 (1975): 741–52, presents a thorough account of the movement in Aquinas's thought on contingency and providence, from the *Commentary on the Sentences of Peter Lombard*, through to the *Summa contra Gentiles*.

9. Quotations from *Summa Contra Gentiles* taken from Bernard J. F. Lonergan, *Grace and Freedom: Operative Grace in the Thought of St. Thomas Aquinas*, ed. Frederick E. Crowe and Robert M. Doran, Collected Works of Bernard Lonergan, vol. 1 (Toronto: University of Toronto Press, 2000).

10. Or as Lonergan pithily summarizes, "what providence intends to be contingent will inevitably be contingent" (ibid, 109). See also the document of the International Theological Commission, "Communion and Stewardship: Human Persons Created in the Image of God," http://www.vatican.va/roman_curia/congregations/cfaith/cti_documents/rc_con_cfaith_doc_20040723_communion-stewardship_en.html.

11. Martin J. Rees, *Just Six Numbers: The Deep Forces That Shape the Universe* (New York: Basic, 2000), 131.

12. See our discussion of this in ch. 1.

13. Bracken, "Response to Elizabeth Johnson," 729–30.

14. Of course, in their own time frame they are decaying at exactly the same rate!

15. This example is taken from Brian Greene, *The Fabric of the Cosmos: Space, Time, and the Texture of Reality* (New York: Knopf, 2004), 134–38. This is an example of a parallax effect. Small changes in measurement at one place have a large impact of measurements at large distances. Only here the differences are spatio-temporal, not just spatial.

16. Ibid., 139.

17. Ibid., 141.

18. Paul Davies, *The Goldilocks Enigma: Why Is the Universe Just Right for Life?* (London: Allen Lane, 2006), 227.

19. Of course, there are enormous difficulties in marrying general relativity with quantum mechanics. No accepted unification has so far been found, though "string theory" is the most promising account to date. See Brian Greene, *The Elegant Universe: Superstrings, Hidden Dimensions, and the Quest for the Ultimate Theory* (London: Jonathan Cape, 1999).

20. These are thought of as particle and antiparticle pairs that "appear" and annihilate one another before their existence can be detected.

21. For details, see http://www.scientificamerican.com/article.cfm?id=what-is-the
-casimir-effec and http://www.scientificamerican.com/article.cfm?id=are-virtual-particles
-rea.

22. For a fascinating account see Greene, *Elegant Universe.*

23. Augustine, *Saint Augustine on Genesis* (Washington, DC: Catholic University of
America Press, 1991), 50.

24. For example, the *Back to the Future* films or the more recent reboot of the *Star
Trek* film series.

25. A full account of the issues and personalities can be found at http://www.hedweb
.com/everett/everett.htm.

26. Rees, *Just Six Numbers,* 148–54. This approach has been popularized in string
theory. See Greene, *Elegant Universe,* 366–70.

27. For a thorough account of this view, known as "the anthropic principle," see John
D. Barrow and Frank J. Tipler, *The Anthropic Cosmological Principle* (New York: Oxford
University Press, 1988).

28. Either these different worlds are causally disconnected, that is, they cannot affect
one another, in which case they are empirically unverifiable in principle; or they are causally
connected, in which case they are actually part of the same universe after all.

CHAPTER 4. EVOLVING WORLD: PURPOSE AND MEANING

1. When we ask questions about the purpose of some phenomenon we are in the area
of philosophy called "teleology." Although this term itself was only coined in 1740, the
notion that things could be explained by the "end" or, in Greek, the *telos,* toward which
they were oriented, goes back to the ancient world. There are many ways of conceiving
what drives a thing toward its end, but for our concerns the issue is that appeals to an
"end" as an explanation of why something works the way it does have fallen out of favor
in the modern scientific endeavor. In particular, many assume that after Darwin's appeal
to chance teleological explanations are moribund. In this chapter we will explore the many
versions of teleology abroad in the nineteenth century, their demise in the twentieth century,
and recent efforts to revive a new kind of dynamic teleology in line with evolutionary
science.

2. The full reference is William Paley, *Natural Theology, or Evidences of the Existence
and Attributes of the Deity Collected from the Appearance of Nature* (London: Faulder, 1802).

3. In fact, worldviews are seldom challenged head on. As we will discuss later in this
chapter, there is a give and take between scientific discoveries on the ground and the overarching theoretical or metaphysical assumptions that carry weight at a more general level.

4. Charles Lyell (1797–1895) had introduced such new ideas in his three-volume
work, *Principles of Geology, Being an Attempt to Explain the Former Changes of the Earth's
Surface* (London: John Murray, 1830–1833). In fact, Darwin had read the first volume
before he left for his round the world journey on the HMS Beagle and received the second
volume en route. Thus he had read Lyell's novel ideas about changing geological eras as he
encountered a variety of geological forms on his travels. Eventually, Lyell became a close

friend and confidant, though Lyell himself had trouble accepting the implications of Darwin's theory for human evolution.

5. See David Depew and Bruce Weber, *Darwinism Evolving: Systems Dynamics and the Genealogy of Natural Selection* (Cambridge: MIT Press, 1995), 43ff. The drama of conflicting worldviews of science, politics, and philosophy unfolded here between Lamarck and Cuvier in the late eighteenth century.

6. See ibid., 45.

7. He also believed in the agency of organisms—that choices they made which improved their lives in this current existence could and would be passed on to future generations.

8. "Epigenetic" in its broadest meaning simply indicates the idea that something develops from an unformed state toward its adult state. While we take this for granted today, this idea contrasted in the nineteenth century with the idea that embryos were simple mini-adults, fully formed, that grew bigger in gestation.

9. Darwin surely knew how revolutionary his views were. This accounts for the long delay in his publication of his theory of natural selection. He returned from his voyage on the HMS Beagle in 1835, but did not publish *The Origin of Species* till 1859. For more on this delay, see Depew and Weber, *Darwinism Evolving*, 72ff.

10. See ibid., 70–71.

11. Although Gregor Mendel (1822–1884), the Austrian monk now considered the father of modern genetics, was a contemporary of Darwin's, Darwin knew nothing of his work. Indeed, Mendel's work was unknown in his time and only rediscovered in the early twentieth century.

12. Thomas R. Malthus, *An Essay on the Principle of Population, as It Affects the Future Improvement of Society, with Remarks on the Speculations of Mr. Goodwin, M. Condorcet, and Other Writers* (London: J. Johnson, 1898). Darwin mentions this great insight in an entry for September 28, 1838, in his autobiography. Note that Malthus was not a biologist but a political economist.

13. Charles Darwin, *The Autobiography of Charles Darwin*, ed. N. Barlow (London: Collins, 1958), 120, as quoted in Depew and Weber, *Darwinism Evolving*, 71.

14. Depew and Weber summarize the heart of Darwin's theory as follows: "The basic idea is simplicity itself. If it is an inherent, lawlike tendency for organisms to reproduce at rates higher than the means of supporting them, then the resulting competition will be ubiquitous not only between species but among individuals within species. Under these conditions, variant traits that enable their possessors to command more resources, and so to live to reproduce more effectively than their competitors, will, if they are heritable, gradually mold lineages whose adaptedness to their niches is a result of constant reequilibration between organisms and environments. Increasing differences between lineages—races, species, and higher taxa—reflect the fact that organisms under this kind of pressure will tend to explore and exploit new and different resource bases, making them different as well" (*Darwinism Evolving*, 72).

15. Many of Darwin's mentors disagreed with him on this, including Malthus and Lyell. See ibid., 507n4.

16. For a narrative and analysis of the responses to Darwin's work, see ibid., ch. 4. See also Frank M. Turner, "The Victorian Conflict between Science and Religion: A Professional Dimension," *Isis* 49 (1978): 356–76.

17. Depew and Weber make the following comment: "The catalytic effect of Darwin's book, accordingly, was to allow the older tradition of evolutionary thought from which Darwin had tried to keep his distance to rise again. What Darwin feared might happen, did happen. What he did not anticipate was that the old evolutionism once so redolent with revolutionary overtones, would become so respectable or that it would travel under his name" (*Darwinism Evolving*, 171).

18. Ibid., 172. See their entire ch. 7 on the late nineteenth century.

19. See ibid., ch. 12.

20. See ibid., ch. 13.

21. See ibid., 172–76.

22. This graphic view of evolution is strikingly different from what Darwin had envisioned. He saw the relationship of species more like a bush, with many branches and sub-branches, with human emergence as merely one branch among others.

23. This assumption of directionality survived without any necessary reference to divine providence. See ibid., 178–79.

24. Taken from http://commons.wikimedia.org/wiki/File:Pedigree_of_Man_English.jpg.

25. The word *statistics* comes from keeping track of the state of the state. Depew and Weber, *Darwinism Evolving*, 204.

26. R. A. Fischer (1890–1962) began applying such math to gene pools and population genetics emerged. On the probability revolution and its role in theories of evolution see ibid., ch. 8.

27. Jacques Monod, *Chance and Necessity: An Essay on the Natural Philosophy of Modern Biology* (New York: Vintage, 1972), 180. The reference to the watchmaker being blind comes from the title of Richard Dawkins's *The Blind Watchmaker: Why the Evidence of Evolution Reveals a Universe without Design* (New York: Norton, 1996).

28. Bernard J. F. Lonergan, *Insight: A Study of Human Understanding*, ed. Frederick E. Crowe and Robert M. Doran, Collected Works of Bernard Lonergan, vol. 3 (Toronto: University of Toronto Press, 1992), 600.

29. This is, of course, a simplified account. Mendeleev also noted certain periodic patterns among the elements according to their chemical properties. This actually allowed him not only to predict the existence of some missing elements but also to suggest their chemical properties.

30. See http://public.web.cern.ch/public/en/science/StandardModel-en.html.

31. See http://public.web.cern.ch/public/en/Science/Higgs-en.html.

32. The classic work on how scientific paradigms shift along with culture is Thomas S. Kuhn, *The Structure of Scientific Revolutions*, 2d ed. (Chicago: University of Chicago Press, 1970). See discussion of Kuhn and others on science and cultural horizons, Depew and Weber, *Darwinism Evolving*, 21–24.

33. Depew and Weber, *Darwinism Evolving*, 23.

34. Ian Hacking, *The Taming of Chance* (Cambridge: Cambridge University Press, 1990).

35. This discussion is taken from Lonergan, *Insight*, ch. 15, esp. 470–76.

36. Ibid., 497, 477.

37. This determination comes with what Lonergan calls the "virtually unconditioned." The conditions that need to be fulfilled are fulfilled such that we can come to a definitive conclusion. In this way, the indeterminate drive to understand becomes determinate, finality finds its goal in actually knowing something.

38. See http://www.ruf.rice.edu/~bioslabs/studies/invertebrates/dicty.html for details.

39. http://www.metamicrobe.com/dicty/.

40. For a wonderful reflection on the durability but vulnerability of a wildflower named *Silphium*, see Aldo Leopold, *A Sand County Almanac* (New York: Ballantine, 1966 [1949]), 48–54.

41. As we will see later in this chapter, these are systems on "the edge of chaos"—stable but fragile—thus open to emendation. Scholars also use the term "far from equilibrium" to denote a system that is not at rest (in contrast, for example, to a ball that rolls around in a bowl and ultimately comes to rest in the bottom) but is fluid enough to exchange energy and morph into something else.

42. See http://hyperphysics.phy-astr.gsu.edu/hbase/particles/proton.html.

43. Lonergan goes so far as to say that there are no things in things. If the nucleus is a thing (unity identity whole) then it does not contain neutrons and protons, but the schemes of recurrence that were the constitutive neutrons and protons are incorporated into a new and higher scheme of recurrence which modifies the lower schemes significantly.

44. For example, the extinction of the dinosaurs sixty-five million years ago set the stage for the burgeoning of mammalian life.

45. Lonergan would say that evolutionary theories are about the emergence and survival (or not) of schemes of recurrence. That is, evolutionary theory is not about the emergence of organisms or species but about the schemes that allow these to flourish or go extinct. This information comes from an unpublished ms. by philosophy professor Patrick H. Byrne, "What Is Evolutionary Explanation?—Darwin and Lonergan."

46. See Lonergan, *Insight*, 475, where he mentions this "classical illustration" from the work of Hans Driesch on sea urchins. For more on this see http://embryo.asu.edu/view/embryo:123970. See also discussion of Driesch in Depew and Weber, *Darwinism Evolving*, 230, 413–14.

47. Stuart A. Kauffman's major work on these issues is *The Origins of Order: Self-Organization and Selection in Evolution* (New York: Oxford University Press, 1993). We will be depending on a book he wrote for a more general audience, *At Home in the Universe: The Search for Laws of Self-Organization and Complexity* (New York: Oxford University Press, 1995).

48. Depew and Weber, *Darwinism Evolving*, 437.

49. Kauffman, *At Home*, 62.

50. Ibid., 81.

51. Ibid., 82–83.

52. Ibid., 87. It seems that evolution has actually fine tuned this order for free so that "edge of chaos" systems are selected for. In other words, natural selection eliminates systems that are not malleable by natural selection.

53. Kauffman acknowledges the heuristic nature of his work when he says, "The NK model is merely a toy world to tune our intuitions" (ibid., 205).

54. See ibid., 185–89.

55. Sean B. Carroll, *Endless Forms Most Beautiful: The New Science of Evo Devo and the Making of the Animal Kingdom* (New York: Norton, 2005).

56. See http://www.ornl.gov/sci/techresources/Human_Genome/faq/faqs1.shtml# genetics.

57. Early predictions were for 100,000 human genes. In fact, this is the number that Kauffman used throughout his computational models in the 1990s. *At Home in the Universe* was published in 1995, prior to the mapping of the human genome.

58. See Carroll, *Endless Forms*, 79. See also http://www.ornl.gov/sci/techresources/ Human_Genome/faq/compgen.shtml.

59. See ibid., ch. 6.

60. Sean Carroll makes this summary: "The surprising message from Evo Devo is that all of the genes for building large, complex animal bodies long predated the appearance of those bodies in the Cambrian Explosion. The genetic potential was in place for at least 50 million years, and probably a fair bit longer, before large complex forms emerged. This means that while the genetic tool kit was not evolving, the rapid appearance of and changes in body forms tell us that animal development was evolving a great deal" (ibid., 139).

61. Ibid., 111.

62. On the new developmentalism, see Depew and Weber, *Darwinism Evolving*, ch. 15. On Kauffman and his work, see ibid., ch. 16.

63. See Simon Conway Morris, *The Crucible of Creation: The Burgess Shale and the Rise of Animals* (New York: Oxford University Press, 1998).

64. This is an oft-cited comment of Stephen Jay Gould, *Wonderful Life: The Burgess Shale and the Nature of History* (New York: Norton, 1989).

65. Simon Conway Morris, *Life's Solution: Inevitable Humans in a Lonely Universe* (Cambridge: Cambridge University Press, 2003), xii.

66. Note the difference between *convergence* and *co-evolution*. Convergence is when similar traits evolve independently of any common lineage. Co-evolution is when two species or more evolve in relation to one another—predator and prey adapt to each other as they adapt to their environments.

67. See Conway Morris, *Life's Solution*, 295ff. Note: Conway Morris does not cite Kauffman nor indicate any knowledge of his work.

68. Ibid., 302.

69. On the demise of "vitalism" with regard to teleology, see ibid., 5.

70. Ibid., 327.

71. See ibid., 329.

72. Depew and Weber, *Darwinism Evolving*, 476.

73. Ibid., 477–78.

CHAPTER 5. HUMAN FREEDOM AND GOD'S PROVIDENCE

1. Robin Ryan, *God and the Mystery of Human Suffering: A Theological Conversation across the Ages* (New York: Paulist, 2011), 1–2.

2. Indeed, there is an area of study referred to as "cosmic eschatology," the study of the fate of the physical universe. For a speculative example, see Frank J. Tipler, *The Physics of Immortality: Modern Cosmology, God, and the Resurrection of the Dead* (New York: Anchor, 1994).

3. See John D. Barrow and Frank J. Tipler, *The Anthropic Cosmological Principle* (New York: Oxford University Press, 1988), for myriad examples of such fine tuning for life in the universe. Also Paul Davies, *The Goldilocks Enigma: Why Is the Universe Just Right for Life?* (London: Allen Lane, 2006).

4. Hydrogen itself is the direct product of the Big Bang and emerged in the first milliseconds of the universe's existence.

5. This sense of contingency has been a theme in films such as *Sliding Doors* and *The Adjustment Bureau*. In each case small changes have a potentially large impact on the characters involved.

6. Lonergan talks about the explanatory power of large time frames and large numbers of occasions: "low probabilities are offset by large numbers of occasions, so that what is probable only once in a million occasions is to be expected a million times on a million million occasions. In like manner, the rarity of occasions is offset by long intervals of time, so that if the occasions arise only once in a million years, still they arise a thousand times in a thousand million years. At once emerges the explanatory significance of statistical laws. Why are there in the world of our experience such vast numbers and such enormous intervals of time? Because probabilities are low, numbers have to be large; because occasions are rare, time intervals have to be long." Bernard J. F. Lonergan, *Insight: A Study of Human Understanding*, ed. Frederick E. Crowe and Robert M. Doran, Collected Works of Bernard Lonergan, vol. 3 (Toronto: University of Toronto Press, 1992), 136–37.

7. The phrase is used in Alfred Lord Tennyson's poem, *In Memoriam A. H. H.* It has made a regular appearance in debates on evolution.

8. The notion that God must create the "best of all possible worlds" would appear to be vacuous. "Better" and "worse" are relative terms. Any finite reality could always be better, simply because it is not infinite being (God). God does not create the "best" of all possible worlds, simply a world that Genesis affirms is good.

9. This type of position was in fact held by some scientists prior to Darwin, as noted in the previous chapter.

10. Some have suggested divine action at the quantum level, where God manipulates events toward certain outcomes; cf. John Polkinghorne, *Science and Providence: God's Interaction with the World* (Boston: New Science Library, 1989). This again reduces God to the level of a secondary cause and fails to recognize that God is outside the temporal flow. As primary cause God has no need to manipulate reality at any level.

11. M. Scott Peck, *People of the Lie: The Hope for Healing Human Evil* (New York: Simon & Schuster, 1983), 45.

12. Augustine, *The Confessions*, trans. Maria Boulding (New York: Vintage, 1998), 68.

13. Ibid., 69.

14. Ibid., 72.

15. Ibid., 73.

16. Herbert McCabe, *God Matters* (New York: Continuum, 2005), 29.

17. In this way the mystery of evil is very different from what are called the mysteries of faith. Evil lacks intelligibility or meaning. The mysteries of faith are full of intelligibility or meaning, more than we can comprehend.

18. See the article by Jeremy Wilkins, "Grace and Growth: Aquinas, Lonergan, and the Problematic of Habitual Grace," *Theological Studies* 72 (2011): 723–49. Also ch. 6 of Neil Ormerod and Shane Clifton, *Globalization and the Mission of the Church*, ed. Gerard Mannion, Ecclesiological Investigations (London: T & T Clark, 2009).

19. See the Vatican II Pastoral Constitution of the Church, *Gaudium et spes*, n.16. "In the depths of his conscience, man detects a law which he does not impose upon himself, but which holds him to obedience. Always summoning him to love good and avoid evil, the voice of conscience when necessary speaks to his heart: do this, shun that. For man has in his heart a law written by God; to obey it is the very dignity of man; according to it he will be judged. Conscience is the most secret core and sanctuary of a man. There he is alone with God, Whose voice echoes in his depths." See http://www.vatican.va/archive/hist_councils/ ii_vatican_council/documents/vat-ii_const_19651207_gaudium-et-spes_en.html.

20. This is beautifully captured in the children's movie *The Neverending Story*, when one of the characters proclaims that "A strange sort of Nothing is destroying everything."

21. Bernard J. F. Lonergan, *Method in Theology* (London: Darton, Longman & Todd, 1972), 117.

22. For a fuller discussion see Lonergan, *Insight*, ch. 20.

23. For more on this, see McCabe, *God Matters*, ch. 8; Sebastian Moore, *The Crucified Jesus Is No Stranger* (New York: Seabury, 1977); Cynthia S. W. Crysdale, *Embracing Travail: Retrieving the Cross Today* (New York: Continuum, 2001); Neil Ormerod, *Creation, Grace, and Redemption* (Maryknoll, NY: Orbis, 2007), ch. 5.

24. The script is available at http://sfy.ru/?script=gandhi.

CHAPTER 6. **IMPLICATIONS FOR HUMAN LIVING: MORAL AGENCY AND EMERGENT PROBABILITY**

1. See http://www.pbs.org/wgbh/nova/evolution/becoming-human-part-2.html.

2. In fact, just whether the Neanderthals were our relatives was one of the questions this research sought to answer. It seems that some *Homo sapiens*—the direct ancestors of modern humans—did interbreed with Neanderthals, but that the two lines had diverged much, much earlier in human evolution. See Sean B. Carroll, *Endless Forms Most Beautiful: The New Science of Evo Devo and the Making of the Animal Kingdom* (New York: Norton, 2005), 260–61.

3. As quoted in ibid., 250.

4. See ibid., 250, 269.

5. We take it for granted that we are the only human species on earth. But it is interesting to imagine our world if, as in most of human history, several hominin species

coexisted today. Just as there are many canine and feline species, there easily could have been multiple hominin species that perdured to the current time.

6. We must also note, however, that hominin evolution is itself a mere fraction of the 3.8 billion years since life emerged on earth. http://www.bbc.co.uk/nature/history _of_the_earth. For more on human evolution in general, see https://humanorigins.si.edu/ human-characteristics.

7. See Carroll, *Endless Forms*, 259–60.

8. This is adapted from ibid, 259.

9. It is a bit hard to conceive of decimal divisions of millions of years. To convert these to full numbers one simply moves the decimal point 6 spaces to the right. Thus, .3 MYA is 300,000 years ago and .03 MYA is 30,000 years ago.

10. Note that even though the Neanderthal's brain was larger than that of our own species, so was his/her body. What counts is brain size *relative to* body size. Merely having large brains, as many mammals do, does not seem to indicate greater differentiation and expanded adaptation.

11. See http://www.pbs.org/wgbh/nova/evolution/becoming-human-part-3.html.

12. For more on evolution at the molecular level and the distinctively human genetic heritage, see Carroll, *Endless Forms*, 271–76.

13. Quoted in ibid., 261.

14. The recognition of this special role of humans in evolution can be traced back to shortly after Darwin and has a mixed legacy. "Sociobiology" has been tied to various eugenics movements over the last 150 years. For example, see Walt Anderson, *To Govern Evolution: Further Adventures of the Political Animal* (Boston: Harcourt Brace Jovanovich, 1987); Howard L. Kaye, *The Social Meaning of Modern Biology: From Social Darwinism to Sociobiology* (New Brunswick, NJ: Transaction, 1997); and Michael Ruse, *Monad to Man: The Concept of Progress in Evolutionary Biology* (Cambridge: Harvard University Press, 1996).

15. For more on individual, group, and general bias, see Bernard J. F. Lonergan, *Insight: A Study of Human Understanding*, ed. Frederick E. Crowe and Robert M. Doran, Collected Works of Bernard Lonergan, vol. 3 (Toronto: University of Toronto Press, 1992), 244–69. These power differentials and biases are what, in the end, made any hopeful expectations of eugenics deteriorate into the horrors of Hitler's "experiments."

16. Sharon D. Welch, *A Feminist Ethic of Risk* (Minneapolis: Fortress Press, 1990). A revised edition of this book was published in 2000. The changes involve revisions to one particular chapter, "The Ethic of Control," where she had discussed the nuclear-arms policies of the 1980s. In the process, however, she has deleted much of her earlier description of an ethic of control. Thus, unless otherwise noted, the quotations here are from the original version of 1990.

17. Ibid., 25.

18. Ibid., 23.

19. Ibid.

20. Paule Marshall, *The Chosen Place, the Timeless People* (New York: Vintage, 1984), 175–81. See the discussion of this in Welch, *Feminist Ethic*, 57–58 (both editions).

21. Welch, *Feminist Ethic*, 19 (2d ed., 45).

22. Ibid., 20 (2d ed., 46).

23. Ibid.

24. Recall the example of finality used in ch. 4, which involved human curiosity pushing us to ask questions in a directed way without determining outcomes prior to our asking and answering of questions. This exposition is an extension of that discussion.

25. Lonergan would say that judgments of fact are complete when reflection reaches a "virtually unconditioned." That is to say, the conditions necessary for the judgment to be true are fulfilled. See Lonergan, *Insight*, 280–89.

26. Mildred D. Taylor, *Roll of Thunder, Hear My Cry*, 25th ann. ed. (New York: Dial, 2001), 40–41, as quoted in Welch, *Feminist Ethic*, 72–73.

27. Alston Chase, *Playing God in Yellowstone: The Destruction of America's First National Park* (San Diego: Harcourt Brace Jovanovich, 1987), 24–25. Chase tells this tale as a shorter and simpler example of what unfolded in Yellowstone National Park over a sixty-year period with elk herds. Australia has a number of cases of such ecological disasters arising from human intervention. Two notable ones are the following: the introduction of the rabbit, which had no natural predators and has caused inestimable damage to farming land and the natural environment in Australia; and the introduction of the cane toad, ostensibly as a means of biological control, into the sugar cane fields of Queensland. It has since spread through vast regions of Australia, damaging natural wildlife with its toxic excretions.

28. Jonathan Weiner, *The Beak of the Finch* (New York: Vintage, 1995), 258.

29. As quoted in ibid.

30. Harold Neu, as discussed and quoted in ibid., 265.

31. Ibid., 265–66.

32. This story was aired on CBC television (*The National*) as a documentary made by Grant Gelinas entitled "Nicole's Dream." It appeared on Sept. 21, 2006, and aired again on Jan. 1, 2007. More information about the group started by Nicole Pageau in Edmonton can be found at http://www.ubuntuedmonton.org/en/about.htm.

33. For more on this see Rosemary Haughton, *The Transformation of Man: A Study of Conversion and Community* (London: Geoffrey Chapman, 1967). See also Cynthia S. W. Crysdale, "Heritage and Discovery: A Framework for Moral Theology," *Theological Studies* 63 (2002): 559–78.

CONCLUSION. CAN A TRANSCENDENT GOD BE A PERSONAL GOD?

1. For example, Elizabeth A. Johnson, *Quest for the Living God: Mapping Frontiers in the Theology of God* (New York: Continuum, 2007).

2. Bernard J. F. Lonergan, *Insight: A Study of Human Understanding*, ed. Frederick E. Crowe and Robert M. Doran, Collected Works of Bernard Lonergan, vol. 3 (Toronto: University of Toronto Press, 1992).

3. Brian Greene, *The Fabric of the Cosmos: Space, Time, and the Texture of Reality* (New York: Knopf, 2004).

4. Paul Davies, *The Goldilocks Enigma: Why Is the Universe Just Right for Life?* (London: Allen Lane, 2006).

5. Martin J. Rees, *Just Six Numbers: The Deep Forces That Shape the Universe* (New York: Basic, 2000), 131.

6. This is the classical notion of God as "pure act" or *actus pura*.

7. For the full formulation: "In agreement, therefore, with the holy fathers, we all unanimously teach that we should confess that our Lord Jesus Christ is one and the same Son, the same perfect in Godhead, the same perfect in humanity, truly God and truly human, the same of a rational soul and body, consubstantial with the Father in Godhead, and the same consubstantial with us in humanity, like us in all things except sin; begotten from the Father before the ages as regards his Godhead, and in the last days, the same, because of us and because of our salvation begotten from the Holy Virgin, the Theotokos, as regards His humanity; one and the same Christ, Son, Lord, only-begotten, made known in two natures, without confusion, without change, without divisions, without separations, the difference of the natures being by no means removed because of the union, but the property of each nature being preserved and coalescing in one *prosopon* and one *hypostasis*—not parted or divided into two *prosopa*, but one and the same Son, only begotten, divine Word, the Lord Jesus Christ, as the prophets of old and Jesus Christ himself have taught us about Him and the creed of our fathers has handed down" (adapted from http://www.ewtn.com/faith/teachings/incac2.htm). Note the clear distinction between the two natures, human and divine, each of which maintains fully all their defining properties.

BIBLIOGRAPHY

Anderson, Walt. *To Govern Evolution: Further Adventures of the Political Animal.* Boston: Harcourt Brace Jovanovich, 1987.

Augustine. *The Confessions.* Trans. Maria Boulding. New York: Vintage, 1998.

———. *Saint Augustine on Genesis.* Trans. Roland J. Teske. Washington, DC: Catholic University of America Press, 1991.

Ayala, Francisco J. "Intelligent Design: The Original Version." *Theology and Science* 1 (2003): 9–32.

———. *Darwin and Intelligent Design.* Facets series. Minneapolis: Fortress Press, 2006.

Barbour, Ian G. *Religion and Science: The Historical and Contemporary Issues.* San Francisco: HarperCollins, 1997.

———. *When Science Meets Religion.* San Francisco: HarperSanFrancisco, 2000.

Barrow, John D., and Frank J. Tipler. *The Anthropic Cosmological Principle.* New York: Oxford University Press, 1988.

Bartholomew, David J. *God, Chance, and Purpose: Can God Have It Both Ways?* Cambridge: Cambridge University Press, 2008.

Behe, Michael J. *Darwin's Black Box: The Biochemical Challenge to Evolution.* 10th ann. ed. New York: Free, 2006.

———. *The Edge of Evolution: The Search for the Limits of Darwinism.* New York: Free Press, 2007.

Bohm, David. *Wholeness and the Implicate Order.* Routledge Classics. London: Routledge, 2002.

Bracken, Joseph A. "Response to Elizabeth Johnson's 'Does God Play Dice?' " *Theological Studies* 57 (1996): 720–30.

Buckley, Michael J. *At the Origins of Modern Atheism.* New Haven: Yale University Press, 1987.

Byrne, Patrick. "Lonergan, Evolutionary Science, and Intelligent Design." *Revista Portuguesa de Filosofia* 63 (2007): 893–913.

———. "Quaestio Disputata: Evolution, Randomness, and Divine Purpose: A Reply to Cardinal Schonborn." *Theological Studies* 67 (2006): 653–65.

Carroll, Sean B. *Endless Forms Most Beautiful: The New Science of Evo Devo and the Making of the Animal Kingdom*. New York: Norton, 2005.

Chase, Alston. *Playing God in Yellowstone: The Destruction of America's First National Park*. San Diego: Harcourt Brace Jovanovich, 1987.

Conway Morris, Simon. *The Crucible of Creation: The Burgess Shale and the Rise of Animals*. New York: Oxford University Press, 1998.

———. *Life's Solution: Inevitable Humans in a Lonely Universe*. Cambridge: Cambridge University Press, 2003.

Crysdale, Cynthia S. W. *Embracing Travail: Retrieving the Cross Today*. New York: Continuum, 1999.

———. "Heritage and Discovery: A Framework for Moral Theology." *Theological Studies* 63 (2002): 559–78.

———. "Making a Way by Walking: Risk, Control, and Emergent Probability." *Théoforum* 39 (2008): 39–58.

———. "Playing God? Moral Agency in an Emergent World." *Journal of the Society of Christian Ethics* 23 (2003): 398–426.

———. "Risk Versus Control: Grounding a Feminist Ethic for the New Millennium." In *Themes in Feminist Theology for the New Millennium (III)*, ed. Gaile M. Polhaus, 1–22. Villanova: Villanova University Press, 2006.

Darwin, Charles. *The Autobiography of Charles Darwin*. Ed. N. Barlow. London: Collins, 1958.

———. *On the Origin of Species by Means of Natural Selection*. Mineola, NY: Dover Publications, 2006 [1859].

Davies, Paul. "E.T. And God: Could Earthly Religions Survive the Discovery of Life Elsewhere in the Universe?" *The Atlantic Monthly* (September 2003), 112–18.

———. *The Edge of Infinity: Where the Universe Came From and How It Will End*. New York: Simon & Schuster, 1981.

———. *God and the New Physics*. New York: Simon & Schuster, 1983.

———. *The Goldilocks Enigma: Why Is the Universe Just Right for Life?* London: Allen Lane, 2006.

———. *The Last Three Minutes: Conjectures About the Ultimate Fate of the Universe*. Science Masters Series. New York: Basic, 1994.

————. *The Mind of God: The Scientific Basis for a Rational World.* New York: Simon & Schuster, 2005.

————. "Now Is the Reason for Our Discontent." *Sydney Morning Herald,* 1 January 2003.

Dawkins, Richard. *The Blind Watchmaker: Why the Evidence of Evolution Reveals a Universe without Design.* New York: Norton, 1996.

————. *The God Delusion.* Boston: Houghton Mifflin, 2006.

Dembski, William A. *The Design Revolution: Answering the Toughest Questions About Intelligent Design.* Downers Grove, IL: InterVarsity, 2004.

————. *Intelligent Design: The Bridge Between Science & Theology.* Downers Grove, IL: InterVarsity, 1999.

————, and Sean McDowell. *Understanding Intelligent Design.* Eugene, OR: Harvest House, 2008.

Depew, David J., and Bruce H. Weber. *Darwinism Evolving: Systems Dynamics and the Genealogy of Natural Selection.* Cambridge: MIT Press, 1995.

Edwards, Denis. *The God of Evolution: A Trinitarian Theology.* New York: Paulist, 1999.

————. *Jesus the Wisdom of God: An Ecological Theology.* Maryknoll, NY: Orbis, 1995.

Gould, Stephen Jay. *Wonderful Life: The Burgess Shale and the Nature of History.* New York: Norton, 1989.

Greene, Brian. *The Elegant Universe: Superstrings, Hidden Dimensions, and the Quest for the Ultimate Theory.* London: Jonathan Cape, 1999.

————. *The Fabric of the Cosmos: Space, Time, and the Texture of Reality.* New York: Knopf, 2004.

Hacking, Ian. *The Taming of Chance.* Cambridge: Cambridge University Press, 1990.

Hartshorne, Charles. *Aquinas to Whitehead: Seven Centuries of Metaphysics of Religion.* Milwaukee: Marquette University Press, 1976.

Haughton, Rosemary. *The Transformation of Man: A Study of Conversion and Community.* London: Geoffrey Chapman, 1967.

Johnson, Elizabeth A. "Does God Play Dice? Divine Providence and Chance." *Theological Studies* 57 (1996): 3–18.

————. *Quest for the Living God: Mapping Frontiers in the Theology of God.* New York: Continuum, 2007.

Kauffman, Stuart A. *At Home in the Universe: The Search for Laws of Self-Organization and Complexity.* New York: Oxford University Press, 1995.

——. *The Origins of Order: Self-Organization and Selection in Evolution.* New York: Oxford University Press, 1993.

Kaye, Howard L. *The Social Meaning of Modern Biology: From Social Darwinism to Sociobiology.* New Brunswick, NJ: Transaction, 1997.

Kuhn, Thomas S. *The Structure of Scientific Revolutions.* 2d ed. Chicago: University of Chicago Press, 1970.

Leopold, Aldo. *A Sand County Almanac.* New York: Ballantine, 1966 [1949].

Lonergan, Bernard J. F. *Grace and Freedom: Operative Grace in the Thought of St. Thomas Aquinas.* Ed. Frederick E. Crowe and Robert M. Doran. Collected Works of Bernard Lonergan, vol. 1. Toronto: University of Toronto Press, 2000.

——. *Insight: A Study of Human Understanding.* Ed. Frederick E. Crowe and Robert M. Doran. Collected Works of Bernard Lonergan, vol. 3. Toronto: University of Toronto Press, 1992.

——. *Method in Theology.* London: Darton, Longman, and Todd, 1972.

Lyell, Charles. *Principles of Geology, Being an Attempt to Explain the Former Changes of the Earth's Surface.* London: John Murray, 1830–1833.

Malthus, Thomas R. *An Essay on the Principle of Population, as It Affects the Future Improvement of Society, with Remarks on the Speculations of Mr. Goodwin, M. Condorcet, and Other Writers.* London: J. Johnson, 1898.

Marshall, Paule. *The Chosen Place, the Timeless People.* New York: Vintage, 1984.

Mayr, Enrst. *What Evolution Is.* New York: Basic, 2001.

McCabe, Herbert. *God Matters.* London; New York: Continuum, 2005.

McGinn, Bernard. "The Development of the Thought of Thomas Aquinas on the Reconciliation of Divine Providence and Contingent Action." *Thomist* 39 (1975): 741–52.

McGrath, Alister E. *Dawkins' God: Genes, Memes, and the Meaning of Life.* Malden, MA: Blackwell, 2005.

——, and Joanna McGrath. *The Dawkins Delusion: Atheist Fundamentalism and the Denial of the Divine.* Downers Grove, IL: InterVarsity, 2007.

McShane, Philip. *Randomness, Statistics, and Emergence.* Dublin: Gill & Macmillan, 1970.

Melchin, Kenneth R. *History, Ethics, and Emergent Probability: Ethics, Society, and History in the Work of Bernard Lonergan.* 2nd ed. Ottawa: Lonergan Web Site, 1999. http://www.lonerganresource.com/book.php?6.

Monod, Jacques. *Chance and Necessity: An Essay on the Natural Philosophy of Modern Biology.* New York: Vintage, 1972.

Moore, Sebastian. *The Crucified Jesus Is No Stranger.* New York: Seabury, 1977.

Ormerod, Neil. *Creation, Grace, and Redemption.* Maryknoll, NY: Orbis, 2007.

———, and Shane Clifton. *Globalization and the Mission of the Church.* Ed. Gerard Mannion, Ecclesiological Investigations. London: T & T Clark, 2009.

Paley, William. *Natural Theology, or Evidences of the Existence and Attributes of the Deity Collected from the Appearance of Nature.* London: Faulder, 1802.

Peck, M. Scott. *People of the Lie: The Hope for Healing Human Evil.* New York: Simon & Schuster, 1983.

Polkinghorne, John. *Science and Providence: God's Interaction with the World.* Boston: New Science Library, 1989.

Popper, Karl. *The Logic of Scientific Discovery.* New York: Harper & Row, 1959.

Rees, Martin J. *Just Six Numbers: The Deep Forces That Shape the Universe.* New York: Basic, 2000.

Ruse, Michael. *Monad to Man: The Concept of Progress in Evolutionary Biology.* Cambridge: Harvard University Press, 1996.

Ryan, Robin. *God and the Mystery of Human Suffering: A Theological Conversation across the Ages.* New York: Paulist, 2011.

Schönborn, Christopher. *Chance or Purpose? Creation, Evolution and a Rational Faith.* Trans. Henry Taylor. San Francisco: Ignatius, 2007.

Snobelen, Stephen. "Isaac Newton, Heretic: The Strategies of a Nicodemite." *British Journal of the History of Science* 32 (1999): 381–419.

Taylor, Charles. *Sources of the Self: The Making of the Modern Identity.* Cambridge: Harvard University Press, 1989.

Taylor, Mildred D. *Roll of Thunder, Hear My Cry.* 25th ann. ed. New York: Dial, 2001.

Tipler, Frank J. *The Physics of Immortality: Modern Cosmology, God, and the Resurrection of the Dead.* New York: Anchor, 1994.

Turner, Frank M. "The Victorian Conflict between Science and Religion: A Professional Dimension." *Isis* 49 (1978): 356–76.

Ulanowicz, R. E. *Ecology: The Ascendent Perspective.* New York: Columbia University Press, 1997.

Weiner, Jonathan. *The Beak of the Finch.* New York: Vintage, 1995.

Welch, Sharon D. *A Feminist Ethic of Risk*. 2d ed. Minneapolis: Fortress Press, 2000 (1990).

Whitehead, Alfred North. *Process and Reality: An Essay in Cosmology*. Ed. David Ray Griffin and Donald W. Sherburne. New York: Free, 1978.

Wilkins, Jeremy. "Grace and Growth: Aquinas, Lonergan and the Problematic of Habitual Grace." *Theological Studies* 72 (2011): 723–49.

Williams, Rowan. *On Christian Theology*. Challenges in Contemporary Theology. Malden, MA: Blackwell, 2000.

INDEX

Aquinas, Thomas, 16, 18, 41, 53, 87, 133n26
   on contingency and divine providence, 45, 137n8
   Summa contra Gentiles (SCG) and, 45
adaptation(s), 59, 60, 61, 79, 81, 104, 106, 107, 136n35
   brain/body size in hominin evolution and, 104–105 (table 6.1), 145n10
agnosticism, Paul Davies and, 15–16
AIDS, 112, 118
antibiotics, 117, 118
argument from design, 11, 54, 133n28. *See also* God; teleology
   meaning of, 6
   Richard Dawkins and, 17
Aristotle, 13, 42, 45
   vs. Galilean concepts of cosmos, 14
artificial selection, 60
atheism, 47, 56, 59
   Deism and modern rise of, 131n7
   Richard Dawkins and, 15–17
   vs. theists on special chance of creation, 20
atom(ic), 66, 69, 71, 73, 85
Augustine, 8, 52, 53, 132n8; 138n23; 143nn12, 13; 144nn14, 15
   evil and, 93, 97

authority systems, clash of scientific and religious, 14
Ayala, Francisco, 35, 37
   intelligent design and, 136nn31, 32, 38–41

Baer, Karl Ernst von, 59–60
"Becoming Human" (NOVA documentary), 103
Bible, 8, 41, 125
   fundamentalist interpretation of, 17
biblical, 94
bipedalism, in hominin evolution, 105
Big Bang, 21, 84, 86, 127, 143n4
blind watchmaker, 11, 81, 140n27
Bohm, David, 10, 132n14
Boltzman, Ludwig, 64
Bracken, Joseph, 43–44, 48, 137nn4–6, 13
Brahe, Tycho, 3
brain
   body size in hominin evolution and, 104–105, 106 (table 6.1), 109–110, 145n10
   evolution of, 107
British, 102
   colonialism, 123
   Empire, 101

buttercups (statistical analysis of distribution), 25 (table 2.1), 25–26,
134nn10–11
Byrne, Patrick, 31, 38, 134n17; 135n21;
136n42; 141n45

Cambrian explosion, 78, 79, 142n60
Cape Verde Islands, 60
Carroll, Sean, 75, 78, 142nn55, 58–61;
144nn2–4; 145nn7, 8, 12, 13
Casimir effect, 53
Catholic Church
conflict with Galileo, 1, 3–4, 14
and metaphysics and morality, 13
Catholic Encyclopedia, 8
causality, 34, 38, 116, 121, 123, 124. *See
also* chance
chance, 35, 57, 59, 68, 74, 104, 107,
110, 113, 120, 124, 126, 136n39. *See
also* contingency
emergence of creation and, 19–20
divine providence and, 45, 55–56
natural selection and, 36–39, 65
necessity and, 39, 43, 57, 121, 124
"sheer," 20, 24, 31, 36, 39
Chase, Alston, 116, 146n27
Christian, 7, 8, 10, 18, 43, 45, 56, 100,
108, 128–29
belief and Greek philosophy, 13–14
tradition and natural theology,
133n29
classical science, 124, 126–27. *See also*
modern science; science
decision making and, 113
intersection of statistical science and,
24–25, 31–32
meaning of term, 21–22
and statistical science differentiated,
22–24, 39

climate change, 105–106, 107
"collectively autocatalytic systems"
(Kaufmann), 76
complexity, 77, 79, 81, 87
chance operations and, 136nn39, 40
emergence of, 142n60
increase seen as higher form of life,
135n28
orienting evolutionary purpose, 58
theory, meaning of term, 75
complex systems, meaning of, 75. *See also*
complexity
conditioning. *See also* judgment
environmental, 108
schemes of recurrence and, 33, 73,
135n22; 141n37; 146n25
social, 95
Confessions (Augustine), 93, 143nn12, 13;
144nn14, 15
conscience, 96, 144n19
consciousness, 71
"sensitive consciousness" enabled by
schemes of recurrence, 34, 39
contingency/-ies, 57, 64, 80, 86, 116,
143n5. *See also* chance
divine providence and, 45, 55,
137nn8, 10
necessity and contingent secondary
causes, 47
necessity and, in conceptualization of
God, 42–45
contingent action. *See* contingency
convergence, 6, 74
evolutionary, 80–81
difference between co-evolution and,
142n66
Conway Morris, Simon, 75, 79–80,
142nn63, 65, 67, 68
Stuart Kaufmann and, 142n67

Copernicus, Nicholas, 3, 66
cosmologist, 15, 20, 85, 86
cosmology, 3, 13, 125, 126, 143nn2, 3,
    137n7. *See also* eschatology
Council of Chalcedon, 129
creation, 20, 46, 52, 53, 54, 86, 91, 94,
    98, 100, 124, 125, 126, 127, 128. *See
    also* creator; creation science; God;
    special creation
Big Bang and, 143n4
as "best of all possible worlds," 143n8
chance and, 20, 55
contingent and wholly dependent on
    God, in Thomas Aquinas, 45, 47–48
dynamic, as challenge to deterministic
    teleology, 58–59
fundamentalist interpretation of Gen-
    esis account, 2, 6, 16–17, 88
God's teleological relationship to,
    11–13, 58, 83, 84–85
providence and the goodness of,
    87–90, 95, 101, 129–30
providence, prayer and, 90–91
reconceptualization of God's relation-
    ship to, 39, 41–44
relationship between God, evolution
    and, 2, 9, 15, 17, 19
vs. evolutionary theories, 11, 57, 80
creation science, 17, 46
Creator, 9, 13, 47, 58, 59, 104, 121, 122,
    124, 127
Cuvier, George, 59, 139n5

Daphne Major, study of finches in,
    26–31, 36, 135n29
Darwin, Charles, 7–9, 20–21, 35, 36,
    59, 60, 61, 62, 133nn5, 20; 138n1;
    139nn7, 9–13, 15; 140nn16–22;
    143n9; 145n14. *See also* Darwinism

Charles Lyell and, 138n4
Herbert Spenser and phrase "survival
    of the fittest," 136n34
Thomas Malthus and, 61, 139n12
William Paley and, 58
Darwinism, 64. *See also* evolution; natural
    selection; science
David Depew and Bruce Weber's sum-
    mary of, 81, 139n14
development of, 7–8
evolutionary theory and, 62
neo-Darwinian evolutionary theories,
    38
Newtonian worldview and, 7–9, 10, 60
quantum mechanics and, 7–9
teleology and, 58–65
Davies, Paul, 19–20, 52, 132nn21, 24,
    25; 133nn1–4; 137n18; 143n3;
    146n4
overview of his scientific agnosticism,
    15–16
Richard Dawkins and, 15–17
Dawkins, Richard, 9, 11, 12, 132nn11,
    15, 17, 22, 23; 133nn27, 28; 140n27
overview of his atheism, 15–17
Paul Davis and, 15–17
decision making, 112, 113–16
ethic of control, ethic of risk and, 110
decorative art, 87, 96
in hominin evolution, 107, 109
Deism, 7, 58
atheism and, 131n7
meaning of, 6
Depew, David, and Bruce Weber, 62, 67,
    75, 81, 135n28, 139nn5, 6, 9, 10, 13,
    14, 140nn17–21, 23, 25, 26, 32, 33;
    141nn46, 48; 142nn62, 72, 73
new developmentalism and, 142n62
summary of Darwinism and, 139n14

INDEX

hydrogen atom, 85, 143n4
  Schrödinger's wave equation and,
    9–10

incarnation. *See also* God; Jesus Christ
  of Jesus Christ, 13, 95
  vs. classical theism, 128–29
India, 101, 123
intelligent design, 5, 46
  Francisco Ayala and, 136nn31, 32, 38,
    39, 41
  Paul Davis and, 16
intelligibility of probability, 24. *See
  also* emergent probability; statistical
  science
  emergent probability and, 31–32
intelligibility of system. *See also* emergent
  probability; statistical science
  meaning of term, 24
  intersection with "intelligibility of
    probability" to form emergent
    probability, 31–32
Islam, 108

Jesus Christ, 90, 100, 101, 105, 124. *See
  also* incarnation
  incarnate with human and divine
    nature, 13, 95, 129, 147n7; rela-
    tive to classical theism, 128–29
  suffering of, 129
Job, 84, 88–89
John Paul II (Pope), 13
Johnson, Elizabeth, 43, 137nn4, 13; 146n1
Judaism, 108
Judgment
  of fact, 70
  value, 112, 113–14
  "virtually unconditioned," (Lonergan),
    141n37; 146n25

Jung, Carl, 95

Kaibab peninsula, 116–17
Kauffman, Stuart, 75–76, 77, 78, 79,
  141nn46–51; 142nn52–54, 57, 62
  Simon Conway Morris and, 80,
    142n67
Kepler, Johannes, and laws of planetary
  motion, 3, 4, 66, 67, 132n20
  Isaac Newton's refinement of Kepler's
    laws, 4
Krebs, Hans Adolf, 33, 71–72
Kreb's cycle, 33 (fig. 2.2), 34
  meaning of, 33

Lamarck, Jean-Baptiste, 58, 59, 60,
  139n5
language, 87, 105, 125, 126
  evolution and development of, 109,
    124
Laplace, Pierre-Simon, 5–6, 10
  his determinism as secondary causa-
    tion, in Thomas Aquinas, 47
  philosophical determinism conclu-
    sion, 9
  refinement of Newton's analyses and,
    5–6
Large Hadron Collider, 67, 140n31
lawfulness
  classical and statistical forms of, 39,
    41, 46, 47, 85, 87, 99
  meaning of word, 39
  statistical, 88, 95, 96, 102
lawlike certitude, 20, 24, 31, 34, 36, 39.
  See also chance
  "sheer chance" and, 20, 24, 31, 36, 39
laws of nature, 5, 7, 20, 39
laws of planetary motion. *See also* Kepler;
  Newton

162

derivation of, in Newton's work, 4

Kepler's, 3

Newton's, 4, 6, 8, 49

Leaky, Meave and Richard, 103, 108, 124

Leopold, Aldo, 117, 141n40

light. *See also* time

  in gravitational fields (Einstein), 52

  speed of, and understanding of time
    and space, 49–54

  viewed from Hubble Space Telescope,
    50–51

light years, meaning of, 51

Lonergan, Bernard, 18, 32, 39, 65,
    68, 76, 98, 126, 133n30; 134nn9,
    10; 135nn21, 22, 30; 137nn9, 10;
    140n28; 141nn34–37, 43–46; 143n6;
    144nn21, 22; 145n15; 146nn25, 26

Lucy (*Australopithecus afarensis* specimen),
    105

"luminiferous aether," 49–50

Malthus, Thomas

  Charles Darwin and, 61, 139nn12,
    15

mammals, 85, 104, 107, 141n44; 145n10

Manichaeism, 93

"many-worlds" theory, 54–55

Marshall, Paule, 111, 145n20

matter, 13, 47, 52, 53, 55, 71, 84,
    131nn1, 2

  interrelation of space, time and,
    48–53, 55, 56, 84

Mayr, Ernst, 38, 135n28; 136nn41, 43

Maxwell, James Clarke, 49, 64

McCabe, Herbert, 93, 144n16

Mendel, Gregor, 64, 139n11

Mendeleev, Dmitri, 66, 140n29

metaphysical, 16, 17, 64, 65, 93. *See also*
    metaphysics

convergence with deterministic sci-
    ence, 6

mixed with science and religious
    belief, in Newtonian worldview, 9

morality, evolution and, 12

worldview, 3

metaphysics, 16, 17. *See also* metaphysical

  meaning of, 131n2

  metascience as, 16

metascience. *See* metaphysics

Michelson-Morley experiment, 49–50

migration, 39, 106

  meaning of, 37

modern science, 15, 18, 41, 45, 48, 54,
    56, 84, 101, 125, 126. *See also* classical
    science; science

molecule(s)/molecular, 69, 71, 80,
    145n12

  biology, 62, 68

  emergence of phase transition in,
    75–76

Monod, Jacques, 19–20, 64, 132n10;
    133n2; 140n27

moral action, 13, 111, 112. *See also* moral
    agency; morality

moral agency, 110–15, 122, 123, 124. *See
    also* moral action; morality

morality, 11, 43, 55, 96, 102. *See also*
    ethics; evil; sin

  metaphysics, evolution and, 12–13

mule deer, preservation on Kaibab penin-
    sula, 116–17

"multiverse" theory, 54–55

mutation, 39, 77, 107

  meaning of, 37

natural elimination, 39, 77. *See also* natu-
    ral selection

  meaning of term, 36

Printed in the USA
CPSIA information can be obtained
at www.ICGtesting.com
LVHW011031031023
759950LV00011B/205

9 780800 698775